Naples '44

Naples '44

Norman Lewis

Pantheon Books
New York

Library of Congress Cataloging in Publication Data

Lewis, Norman.
    Naples '44.

    1. World War, 1939-1945—Personal narratives,
English. 2. Lewis, Norman. 3. World War,
1939–1945—Italy—Naples. 4. Naples—History.
5. Great Britain. Army. Field Security
Personnel—Biography. 6. Soldiers—Great Britain
—Biography. I. Title
D811.L432A36   1978b   940.54′81′41   78-13060
ISBN 0-394-50354-6

Manufactured in the United States of America

First American Edition

For All My Old Friends
of Naples. Especially for
Sergio Viggiani

Foreword

Volunteers from the armed forces in World War II found to possess linguistic qualifications, but who had attended either a redbrick university, or no university at all, were frequently directed into the Intelligence Corps. There followed four months of basic infantry training, plus another two at the Corps Depot at Winchester, the latter period largely devoted to ceremonial marching and learning to ride a motor-cycle. Only in a final two weeks at Matlock was any Intelligence instruction imparted. At the end of this fortnight, trainees considered to have shown promise were interviewed by the Selection Officer, who went through a pretence of discussing with them their future. What the trainee did not realize was that however encouraging the report on the major's desk, or promising the dialogue that ensued, his fate had been instantly settled from the moment of the officer's first quick scrutiny of his face. The Selection Officer believed that blue was the colour of Truth. To the blue-eyed trainees, therefore, went the responsible and sometimes glamorous jobs, while the rest were tipped into the dustbin of what was then called the Field Security Police. In this they were confronted with the drudgery of delivering army-style, pay-attention-you-fuckers lectures, of snooping, detested by all, in the vicinity of military installations in the hope of pouncing on unwatchful guards, or discovering significant scraps of paper not properly disposed of by burning, and of making up alarming rumours with which to fill in the emptiness of the weekly report.

The escape from this predicament was a posting to an overseas section. Most of these, composed at first of an officer and eleven NCO's, were located in the principal cities or ports of countries wherever there happened to be British troops. Others, known as Divisional Sections, accompanied the forces in the field.

Vague as their overseas duties first were, FS men tended more and more to be employed primarily as linguists, to bridge the gap between the military and the civilian population. Often the liaison was fumbling and imperfect. Corps selectors were straightforward men of war without patience for linguistic hairsplitting. Rather, for example, than waste Spanish speakers they were sent to Italy, it being agreed that Spanish and Italian looked in print and sounded much the same. It was typical, too, that a Rumanian-speaking friend should find himself incoherent and gesticulating among the Yugoslav partisans (both were Balkan languages), and that the FSO of 91 FS Section with which I went to Algeria should be an authority on Old Norse, but have no French.

The Field Security Service (as it had hastily renamed itself), brand new in its innocence, confronted emergencies that were undreamed of in England and there were no rules to go by. To have received an inkling of the political situation of the country in which we found ourselves would have been useful, but none was given, and we trod the hard road of trial and error. No. 91's first action in Philippeville – after the FSO had assembled the town's notables and lectured them in Latin – was to release from gaol a certain Giuseppe Moreno, who had convinced us that he was a fervent Gaullist victimized for his pro-Allied stand by the Vichy regime. In reality he was the leader of Algeria's emigrant branch of the Sicilian Mafia, and under sentence of death for the murder of a rival. The mistake must have been fairly typical.

Readers of this diary of a year in Naples may be surprised at the evidence of lack of supervision of the activities of FS personnel. The degree of semi-independence we in fact enjoyed varied from section to section, reflecting in part the military situation and in part the temperament of the commanding officer, who might have a taste for adventure or be by nature timorous. The FS life was on the whole a free one, sometimes gloriously so. But it was a freedom that could go to the head. Protected by the general confusion both as to their duties and powers, sergeants sent 'on detachment' into areas too remote for effective control by their headquarters sometimes became a law unto themselves, engaged in spectacular commercial transactions, involved themselves in tribal intrigue, or even, in one case, married the daughter of a Berber chieftain. Such things were possible in the inaccessible mountains of North Africa, but not in Naples, where there were plenty of adventures, but of a different kind.

My own slight knowledge of Adenese bazaar Arabic kept me occupied with the Arabs of North Africa. First there were visits to the dissident Caïds of Petite Kabylie who were planning the insurrection to come, against their French overlords, and who at that stage would have been happy for Algeria to become a British colony. After that, in Tunisia it was roughly a repeat of the situation, with the involvement this time of the Tunisian royal family. It was while I was engaged in secret conversations with one of its members that the moment came for sections to be reformed for the invasion of Italy. On 1 September 1943 I was posted to 312 FSS who had moved up from Constantine to Oran, and had been temporarily attached to HQ staff of the American Fifth Army. On 5 September we sailed in the *Duchess of Bedford*, leaving Mers el Kebir to join the invasion convoy bound for Salerno.

September 8, 1943 (on board Duchess of Bedford off coast of Italy).

It was announced to us at 6.30 p.m. today that an armistice with Italy has been signed and would take effect from tomorrow, when we are due to land at Salerno. It was clear that no one knew what awaited us, although air-raids on part of the convoy make it seem that the Germans are likely to fight on. We were lectured by an Intelligence officer who told us, surprisingly, that despite all the agents we had assumed to be working for us in Italy absolutely no information had come out regarding the situation. It was not even known whether Mussolini's OVRA still existed. The lecture in fact was purposeless, and could have been summed up in a single sentence: 'We know nothing.'

Except for us, all the troops in this ship are Americans. Although we were attached to the Headquarters of the American Fifth Army at their own request, because they possessed no security service of their own, we are cold-shouldered and left to our own devices except by some poker-playing sergeants, probably Mississippi ferry-boat gamblers in civilian life, who remove my poker winnings accumulated in the past year in a half-hour's play.

September 9

Landed on 'Red Beach', Paestum, at 7 p.m. Boatloads had been going ashore all day after a dawn shelling from the ships and a short battle for the beach-head. Now an extraordinary false serenity lay on the landward view. A great sweep of bay, thinly pencilled with sand, was backed with distant mountains gathering shadows in their innumerable folds. We saw the twinkle of white houses in orchards and groves, and distant villages clustered tightly on hill-tops. Here and there, motion-less columns of smoke denoted the presence of war, but the general impression was one of a splendid and tranquil evening in the late summer on one of the fabled shores of antiquity.

We hauled the motor-cycles off the landing-craft, started them easily, and rode up over the wire-mesh laid across the sand, making for the cover of a wood. The corpses of those killed earlier in the day had been laid out in a row, side by side, shoulder to shoulder, with extreme precision as if about to present arms at an inspection by death. We numbered eleven : ten sergeants and a sergeant-major. Captain Cart-wright, the Field Security Officer, badly smashed up in a car crash the day before we embarked, was presumably still in hospital in Oran. We had been given no briefing or orders of any kind, and so far as the Americans were concerned we might as well not have existed. This was the greatest invasion in this war so far – probably the greatest in human history – and the sea was crowded to the horizon with uncountable ships, but we were as lost and ineffective as babes in the wood. No one knew where the enemy was, but the bodies on the beach at least proved he existed. In place of the guns, tanks, armoured cars, barbed wire we had expected to see, all that had been landed in this sector of the beach were pyramids of office equipment for use by Army Headquarters. We had been issued with a Webley pistol and five rounds of ammunition apiece. Most of us had never fired a gun.

As the sun began to sink splendidly into the sea at our back we wandered at random through this wood full of chirping birds and suddenly found ourselves at the wood's edge. We looked out into an open space on a scene of unearthly enchant-ment. A few hundred yards away stood in a row the three perfect temples of Paestum, pink and glowing and glorious in the sun's last rays. It came as an illumination, one of the great experiences of life. But in the field between us and the temple lay two spotted cows, feet in the air. We crept back into the depths of the sheltering wood, burrowed into the undergrowth, and as soon as night fell, slept. At some time during the night I awoke in absolute darkness to the sound of movements through the bushes, then a mutter of voices in which I distinguished German words. The voices died away, and I slept again.

September 10

A warm, calm, morning. We set out to explore a little of our immediate environment and were admiring the splendid husk of the Temple of Neptune when the war came to us in the shape of a single attacking plane. Hearing its approach, we crouched under a lintel. The plane swooped, opened up with its machine-guns, and then passed on to drop a single bomb on the beach before heading off northwards. One of my friends felt a light tap on a pack he was wearing, caused by a spent machine-gun bullet which fell harmlessly to the ground. The experience was on the whole an exhilarating one. We appreciated the contrasts involved and no one experienced alarm.

In our small way we have become seasoned to the hazards of war. Some delicate inbuilt mechanism of the nerves has accepted and acclimatized itself to a relative loss of security, and minor dangers. This happy situation did not apply in the case of some of the American HQ troops we encountered, who were utterly raw and had been shipped out here straight from the eternal peace of places like Kansas and Wisconsin. The state of their nerves constituted a much greater threat than the FW 190 which paid us a visit about once an hour. Armed hill-billies were constantly jumping out from behind a hedge to point their rifles at us and scream a demand for an answer to a password that nobody had bothered to give us.

Our isolation continues. Battles must be going on somewhere, but all we know of them are the rumours picked up when we join the chow-line. At meal times, when the Sergeant-

Major tries to talk to any of the HQ staff, he is waved away, so we are free to come and go exactly as we please, and occupy ourselves as we think fit. My own personal isolation is of a more absolute order – an isolation within isolation – for as a newcomer to the section I am unavoidably something of an outsider. These men I have known little more than one week have been through the North Africa campaign together, and whatever their original incompatabilities, they have long since shaken down to form their own little closed society. When trouble comes they lock their shields together, and keep their heads down. For the moment I am very much of a stranger.

September 11

The Fifth Army Headquarters has moved, and we – helplessly parasitic as we are – with it, to Albanella Station, just south of the Sele river. This is set in a delicate fusion of landscapes : apple orchards full of glowing fruit, vineyards, and olive groves haunted by multitudes of brilliant blue grasshoppers. A few hundred yards away both the road and railway line are carried on a bridge over the river. This, somewhat damaged, is under repair by a team of British engineers, and it is assumed that sooner or later we shall cross it to advance. Fifteen miles or so away to the north a greyish bruise on the otherwise faultless sky indicates a conflict of which we see or hear nothing, and which in our perfumed Arcadia seems remote and unreal.

For all that, an uneasy feeling is beginning to grow that the present unnatural calm cannot last, and that the Fifth Army does not altogether realize what it is doing here. There are still no tanks in sight, no artillery but a few ack-ack guns, and no signs of any defences being prepared. The only urgent activity in our neighbourhood is that of hundreds of soldiers streaming like ants to bring typewriters and filing cabinets up from the beach. Those not occupied in this way hang about in desultory street-corner groups, many of them unshaven.

We get the impression that they have slight confidence in their leaders and we are frequently asked when we expect Montgomery and the Eighth Army to arrive. Unfortunately Montgomery is still a hundred miles away. So far the only evidence of German interest in our presence here is an occasional visitation by five FW 190s. These cause great alarm but do no damage, as their target is the great armada of ships anchored in the bay.

This afternoon we proceeded with our private exploration of the neighbourhood. We are surrounded by a beautiful desolation. All the farms are abandoned, the trees are heavy with apples, and the ripe tomato crop will soon wither. Unhappy animals mooch about looking for water. Two Americans, tired of their packet K rations containing the ham, cheese, biscuits and sweets that seem so desirable to us, chased after a cow that first galloped, then limped, then staggered as they fired innumerable bullets from their pistols into it. Finally they brought it down and hacked off a hindquarter, with which they departed. We took over an empty farmhouse, littered everywhere with the debris of a hasty departure: articles of clothing strewn about, unmade beds, a pink-cheeked doll on the floor. Italian soldiers who had walked away from the war were plodding along the railway line in their hundreds on their way to their homes in the south. Their feet were usually in terrible shape, with blood sometimes oozing through the cracked leather of their boots; they were in tremendous spirits, and we listened to the trail of their laughter and song all through the day. I spoke to one of these and gave him a few pieces of cheese salvaged from K ration packs jettisoned by the thousand after the candies they contain had been removed. In return he presented me with a tiny scrap of tinselly material torn from a strip he pulled from his pocket. This was from the mantle of a miracle-working Madonna in Pompeii, and by carrying it on my person I would be rendered bullet-proof for at least a year. 'You never know when it might come in handy,' he said, and I agreed. I thanked him profusely, and we shook hands and parted.

Lining up for chow this evening we were told by Americans belonging to the 45th Division that they have been ordered by their officers not only to take no German prisoners, but to use the butts of their rifles to beat to death those who try to surrender. I find this almost incredible.

September 12

Suddenly, today, the war arrived with a vengeance. We were sitting outside our farmhouse, reading, sunning ourselves and trying to come to terms with the acrid-tasting wine, when we noticed that a rumble of distant cannonades, present from early morning, seemed suddenly to have come closer. Soon after, a line of American tanks went by, making for the battle, and hardly any time passed before they were back, but now there were fewer of them, and the wild and erratic manner in which they were driven suggested panic. One stopped nearby, and the crew clambered out and fell into one another's arms, weeping. Shortly afterwards there were cries of 'gas', and we saw frantic figures wearing gasmasks running in all directions.

Chaos and confusion broke out on all sides. The story was that there had been a breakthrough by the 16th Panzer Grenadier Division, which struck suddenly in our direction down the Battipaglia road, with the clear intention of reaching the sea at Paestum, wiping out the Fifth Army HQ, and cutting the beach-head in half.

Rumours began to come in thick and fast, the most damaging one being that General Mark Clark was proposing to abandon the beach-head and had asked the Navy for the Fifth Army to be re-embarked. No one we spoke to believed that this operation was feasible, the feeling being that at the first signs of a withdrawal the Germans would simply roll forward and drive us into the sea.

In view of the general confusion, and the absence of precise information of any kind, Sergeant-Major Dashwood decided to send four members of the Section on their motor-cycles to Salerno tomorrow, using a narrow track running along the shore. The hope was that the Field Security Officer might have arrived there by now, and be able to issue the order releasing us from this absurd predicament. It sounded a hazardous adventure for the people concerned, as no one was even quite certain whether or not the Germans had reached the sea at any point between us and the city. They are certainly in solid possession of the main road running parallel with the track.

This afternoon distraught American ack-ack gunners brought down their third Spitfire. This had just flown in from Sicily and, taking off in pursuit of FW 190s, was immediately shot down, while flying at about 300 feet.

September 14

We are in an olive grove two miles south of Albanella Station. The battle for the beach-head has been going on for twenty hours – all through the day and night. Throughout the afternoon the noise of the bombardment strengthened and drowned the happy chorus of the Italians trudging by incessantly down the railway track on their way home. By nightfall the din was tremendous. German tanks coming down the tongue of land between the Sele and Calore rivers and making for Albanella had reached a point just out of sight of our hastily-dug slit trench, possibly a mile and a half away, where they were taking a pasting from the heavy guns of several battleships anchored just offshore. Every time these opened up with salvoes of fifteen-inch shells our uniforms fluttered in the eddies of blast. To the north a great semi-circle of nightscape had taken on a softly pulsating halo spread by a kind of ragged fireworks display, and occasionally a massive explosion opened up like a pink sea-anemone with wavering feelers of fire. At about eleven o'clock an excited American officer dashed up in a jeep. He was distributing light carbines, and we got one apiece with the warning that the failure to return them next day would be treated as a serious military crime. With these weapons, and our ·38 Webley pistols we were ordered to assist in the defence of Army Headquarters against the Mark IV and Tiger tanks that were now rolling towards us. What this officer did not tell us was that he and the rest of the officers were quietly pulling out and abandoning their men.

Outright panic now started and spread among the American troops left behind. In the belief that our position had been infiltrated by German infantry they began to shoot each other, and there were blood-chilling screams from men hit by the bullets.

We crouched in our slit trench under the pink, fluttering leaves of the olives, and watched the fires come closer, and the night slowly passed. Then at 4 a.m. we learned that the Headquarters was to be evacuated after all, and that we were not to be sacrificed. We started up our motor-bikes, kept as close as we could to the armoured car that had brought the news, and by God's mercy avoiding the panic-stricken fire directed from cover at anything that moved, reached this field with its rabble of shocked and demoralized soldiery – officers separated from their men, and men from their officers.

Official history will in due time set to work to dress up this part of the action at Salerno with what dignity it can. What we saw was ineptitude and cowardice spreading down from the command, and this resulted in chaos. What I shall never understand is what stopped the Germans from finishing us off.

September 15

Miraculously Moore, one of the four sergeants sent to Salerno, got back; a hair-raising twelve-mile drive by jeep, round the edge of a battle raging all the way. The FSO had arrived in the town, and we were ordered to leave the motor-cycles and do our best to get into the town by any vehicle that might attempt the run and could be persuaded to take us. After much negotiating Dashwood managed to line up a command car, but at the last moment we were told that there was not enough space to take us. Later we saw the command car depart, loaded up with wine. The cannonading has been going on all day but the din is lessening. Confusion is still intense. Many of the men we see wandering about have no idea where their officers are and have not seen them since the German counter-attack began.

September 17

Attempts by the remaining section members to reach Salerno having been abandoned, I could find nothing to prevent my taking a sight-seeing trip. I therefore motor-cycled up to the hill village of Capaccio, which had always been in sight from the beach-head, presiding with cool if distant charm over the raucous confusion below and representing for me all that was most romantic in the landscape of Southern Italy.

At close quarters its charm was even more pungent; a place of delicately interlocking white masses, and sparkling light. I rode with some caution into a street which could have been almost English, with narrow, picket-fenced front gardens in which grew such recognizable favourites as zinnias and sweet peas. The peace of this place after four days of the racket of warfare was stunning. Two aged women in black gossiped into each other's ear, and a white-bearded old man, a kind of Italian Father Christmas, spoiled by a crinkling, obsequious smile, sat at a table by his garden gate, selling wine. It was immediately clear that the local belief was that the Germans had gone, never to return, because as soon as he spotted me he held up a notice *Vivono gli Alleati*. I pulled up, bought a glass of wine which looked and tasted like ink, and asked him whether there were any Germans about, and he put on a hideous smirk. He got up and beckoned to me to follow him into his cottage, where a uniformed man was sprawled, head on his chest, in a deep chair. This was the first German I had seen, and he was dead. Speaking in some local dialect quite inaccessible to me, the old man tried to explain what had happened. He was clearly accepting responsibility for the German's death, and expected praise and perhaps even a reward. His gestures seemed to claim that he had put poison in the soldier's wine. I couldn't decide whether or not this was a piece of sycophantic bluff.

I pushed him aside and went out. A disgusting old fellow, but a reliable barometer, I suspected, of the Germans' prospects in this particular theatre of war.

September 18

Today in the chow-line we spoke to a paratrooper of the American 509th Parachute Battalion, still numb with resentment following his experiences of the night of the 14th, when he had taken part in the wild and foolish drop of 600 men sent to disrupt communications in the enemy's rear. The objective, he said, had been Avellino bridge and tunnel, but some of the planes had made the drop up to twenty-five miles off target, and others had dropped parachutists on the roofs of high buildings in Avellino itself, from which, unable to disentangle themselves from their gear in time, they had fallen to their deaths. Men such as this survivor are bitterly critical of their leadership.

In the afternoon another cautious excursion a mile or two up to the Battipaglia road. Shortly after crossing the Sele bridge, I saw a number of the German tanks which had almost reached us on the night of the 14th, and had been put out of action by the naval shelling. Several of these lay near, or in tremendous craters. In one case the trapped crew had been broiled in such a way that a puddle of fat had spread from under the tank, and this was quilted with brilliant flies of all descriptions and colours.

September 20

We finally got through by jeep to Salerno, but found a battle still going on in the outskirts of the town. German mortar bombs were exploding in the middle of a small square only a hundred yards from Security Headquarters. Here I saw an ugly sight: a British officer interrogating an Italian civilian, and repeatedly hitting him about the head with a chair; treatment which the Italian, his face a mask of blood, suffered with stoicism. At the end of the interrogation, which had not been considered successful, the officer called in a private of the Hampshires and asked him in a pleasant, conversational sort of manner, 'Would you like to take this man away, and shoot him?' The private's reply was to spit on his hands, and say, 'I don't mind if I do, sir.' The most revolting episode I have seen since joining the forces.

September 21

Having spent all night patrolling the streets of Salerno on the watch for German infiltrators, there was a meeting with Captain Cartwright, his face covered with plaster. The Captain told us that much as he regretted to say that our presence at Paestum served no purpose of any kind, the Section was still officially attached to HQ, American Fifth Army, and a token presence there was essential, so that five of us, including myself, would have to drag ourselves back. Thus, under compulsion, we returned to the lotos-eating life of the beach-head at Paestum. Here we studied the strange bright grasshoppers, we bird-watched, read a little poetry, practised our Italian on fugitive soldiers, studied again the details of the temples, and sometimes strolled to the sea's edge to watch the great parade of ships, and their magnificent and awful retaliation of fire against the few FW 190s which teased and plagued them with their attacks.

This evening for the first time since the landing we were allowed at last to contribute to the war effort. Someone at Army Headquarters reported suspiciously-flashing lights at night in the village of Castello Castelluccia, and someone else remembered the presence of Intelligence personnel in the camp, so we were sent up to make a stealthy Indian approach through the darkness and catch the supposed spy who was presumed to be signalling to the enemy in the hills. We surrounded the village, waited for the light to begin its flashing and then moved in, only to capture a man with a torch on his way to the single outside latrine, used by the entire village.

September 28

Admitted to the American 16th Evacuation Hospital at Paestum with malaria – possibly a recurrence but more likely a re-infection. I was informed by the doctor that the marshes here are still malarial, and the mosquitoes believed to have put paid to the thriving Greek colony of antiquity, as active as ever. Most of the patients have battle wounds, and from several of these I received confirmation of the story I found so hard to believe, that American combat units were ordered by their officers to beat to death Germans who attempted to surrender to them. These men seem very naïve and childlike, but some of them are beginning to question the ethics of this order. One man who surrendered to a German tank crew was simply stripped of his weapons and turned loose because he could not be carried in the tank, and as a result he is naturally a propagandist for what he accepts as the general high standard of German humanity. Another, more lastingly indoctrinated, has announced his intention of strangling the only wounded German in the ward, an 18-year-old Panzer

Grenadier, as soon as he, the American, has the strength to get out of bed. However, the Panzer Grenadier, cheerful and chirpy despite a bad wound, and with enough of a command of English to display an unabashed sense of humour, is making friends all round and rapidly consolidating his position.

This tentful of men – and there must be at least two hundred of them – are a very mixed bag. One, a lay-preacher in civilian life, conducted the nearest possible thing to revivalist prayer meetings in a situation where all members of the congregation were on their backs, and a proportion had tubes feeding into their nostrils or sticking out of the walls of their stomachs. A great deal of hymn-singing went on in competition with bawdy choruses of the Eskimo Nell variety, and there were frequent ecstatic shouts of 'Bless you, brother, are you saved?' and 'Halleluja!'

A tremendous cannonading by a battery of 105 howitzers in a field a couple of hundred yards away went on through the day, and most of the night. In the end most patients got used to this and were no longer disturbed by the crash of nocturnal salvoes. Yet so finely attuned are the nerves to danger that even in a deep sleep I was awakened instantly by the faint, distant whine of shells from Germans 88s as they passed high overhead on their way to the ships in the bay.

October 3

A gale of the kind no one ever expects of Italy blew down our tent in the middle of the night. Pitch darkness, hammering rain, the suffocating weight of waterlogged canvas over mouth and nostrils, muffled cries from all directions. A lake of water flooded in under the beds, and gradually rose to the level of the bottom of the mattress. It was several hours before we could be rescued. All my kit stowed under the bed was lost, and only my camera and notebooks in the drawer of the bed-side table survived. One patient was killed by the main tent-pole falling across his bed.

October 4

Discharged from hospital and kitted out temporarily as an American private with bucket helmet, hip-clinging trousers and gaitered boots, I picked up a lift in an American truck going in the direction of Naples, which had fallen three days before, and where I supposed the section would already be installed. At Battipaglia it was all change, with an opportunity for a close-quarters study of the effects of the carpet bombing ordered by General Clark. The General has become the destroying angel of Southern Italy, prone to panic, as at Paestum, and then to violent and vengeful reaction, which occasioned the sacrifice of the village of Altavilla, shelled out of existence because it *might* have contained Germans. Here in Battipaglia we had an Italian Guernica, a town transformed in a matter of seconds to a heap of rubble. An old man who came to beg said that practically nobody had been left alive, and that the bodies were still under the ruins. From the stench and from the sight of the flies streaming like black smoke into, and out of, the holes in the ground, this was entirely believable. No attempt had even been made to clear the streets of relics of the successful strike. So much so that while standing by the truck talking to the old man I felt something uneven under one foot, shifted my position, and then glancing down realized that what had at first seemed to be a mass of sacking was in fact the charred and flattened corpse of a German soldier.

Thereafter on through Salerno and across the base of the Sorrento peninsula in a second truck. This is a region on which all the guidebooks exhaust their superlatives, and the war had singed and scorched it here and there, and littered the green and golden landscape with the wreckage of guns and tanks, but happily no town had been large enough to warrant the General's calling in his Flying Fortresses. The only visible damage to most villages had been the inevitable sack of the post office by the vanguard of the advancing troops, who seem to have been philatelists to a man. Presently we were in the outskirts of Naples, which took the form of a number of grimy, war-husked towns: Torre Annunziata, Torre del Greco, Resina and Portici, which have grown together to form twelve miles of dismal suburb along the seafront. We made slow progress through shattered streets, past landslides of rubble from bombed buildings. People stood in their doorways, faces the colour of pumice, to wave mechanically to the victors, the apathetic Fascist salute of last week having been converted to the apathetic V-sign of today, but on the whole the civilian mood seemed one of stunned indifference.

Somewhere a few miles short of Naples proper, the road widened into something like a square, dominated by a vast semi-derelict public building, plastered with notices and with every window blown in. Here several trucks had drawn up and our driver pulled in to the kerb and stopped too. One of the trucks was carrying American Army supplies, and soldiers, immediately joined by several from our truck, were crowding round this and helping themselves to whatever they could lay hands on. Thereafter, crunching through the broken glass that littered the pavement, each of them carrying a tin of rations, they were streaming into the municipal building.

I followed them and found myself in a vast room crowded with jostling soldiery, with much pushing forward and ribald encouragement on the part of those in the rear, but a calmer and more thoughtful atmosphere by the time one reached the front of the crowd. Here a row of ladies sat at intervals of about a yard with their backs to the wall. These women were dressed in their street clothes, and had the ordinary well-washed respectable shopping and gossiping faces of working-class housewives. By the side of each woman stood a small pile of tins, and it soon became clear that it was possible to make love to any one of them in this very public place by adding another tin to the pile. The women kept absolutely still, they said nothing, and their faces were as empty of expression as graven images. They might have been selling fish, except that this place lacked the excitement of a fish market. There was no soliciting, no suggestion, no enticement, not even the discreetest and most accidental display of flesh. The boldest of the soldiers had pushed themselves, tins in hand, to the front, but now, faced with these matter-of-fact family-providers driven here by empty larders, they seemed to flag. Once again reality had betrayed the dream, and the air fell limp. There was some sheepish laughter, jokes that fell flat, and a visible tendency to slip quietly away. One soldier, a little tipsy, and egged on constantly by his friends, finally put down his tin of rations at a woman's side, unbuttoned and lowered himself on her. A perfunctory jogging of the haunches began and came quickly to an end. A moment later he was on his feet and buttoning up again. It had been something to get over as soon as possible. He might have been submitting to field punishment rather than the act of love.

Five minutes later we were on our way again. The tins collected by my fellow travellers were thrown to passers-by who scrambled wildly after them. None of the soldiers travelling on my truck had felt inclined to join actively in the fun.

October 6

The city of Naples smells of charred wood, with ruins everywhere, sometimes completely blocking the streets, bomb craters and abandoned trams. The main problem is water. Two tremendous air-raids on August 4 and September 6 smashed up all the services, and there has been no proper water supply since the first of these. To complete the Allies' work of destruction, German demolition squads have gone round blowing up anything of value to the city that still worked. Such has been the great public thirst of the past few days that we are told that people have experimented with sea-water in their cooking, and families have been seen squatting along the sea-shore round weird contraptions with which they hope to distil sea-water for drinking purposes.

The Section has fallen on its feet. I arrived to find that we had been installed in the Palace of the Princes of Satriano at the end of Naples's impressive seafront, the Riviera di Chiaia, in the Piazza Vittoria. The four-storey building is in the Neapolitan version of Spanish baroque, and we occupy its principal floor at the head of a sweep of marble staircase, with high ceilings, decorated with mouldings, glittering chandeliers, enormous wall-mirrors, and opulent gilded furniture in vaguely French-Empire style. There are eight majestic rooms, but no bathroom, and the lavatory is in a cupboard in the kitchen. The view across the square is of clustered palms, much statuary, and the Bay of Naples. The FSO has done very well by us.

At first sight Naples, with the kind of work it is likely to involve, seemed unglamorous compared with North Africa. Gone for ever were the days of forays into the mountains of Kabylie for meetings with the scheming Caïds and the holy men who controlled the tribes, and the secret discussions in the rose arbour in the Palace Gardens of Tunis. Life here, by comparison, promised to be hard-working, sometimes prosaic, and fraught with routines. There were military units by the dozen all round Naples who wished to employ Italian civilians and all of these had to be vetted by us as security risks. Nothing could have been easier than this operation. The Fascist police state kept close tabs on the activities of all its citizens, and we inherited their extensive archives on the top floor of the Questura – the central police office. Ninety-nine per cent of the information recorded there was numbingly unimportant, and revealed as a whole that most Italians lead political lives of utter neutrality, although prone to sexual adventures. In all, the unending chronicles of empty lives. A little more thought and effort would have to be devoted to the investigation of those few hundreds of persons remaining in the city who had been energetic Fascists, and whom – largely depending on our reports – it might be thought necessary to intern.

A suspects file had to be started, and this was a job that fell to me. Section members had already cleared out the German Consulate in Naples, removing from it a car-load of documents, all of which had to be studied. The work was increased as a deluge of denunciations began to flood in. They were delivered in person by people nourishing every kind of grudge, or even shoved into the hands of the sentry at the gate. Some of them were eccentric, including one relating to a priest who was claimed to have arranged shows of blue movies for the commander of the German garrison. Everything – from the grubbiest scrap of paper on which a name had been scrawled, and the single word 'murderer' scribbled beneath, to a scrupulously typed document bearing the seal and signatures of the Comitato di Liberazione – had to be studied and recorded. The labour involved was immense, and exceedingly tedious, and was much complicated by the prevalence in Naples of certain family names – Espositos and Gennaros turn up by the hundred – and by the fact that material supplied by our own authorities for inclusion in the official Black Book was often vague. Quite frequently suspects were not even identified by name, but by such descriptions as 'of medium height', 'age between thirty and forty', 'strikingly ugly', or in one case, 'known to possess an obsessive fear of cats'. However, the work went on; the filing system expanded, and the Black Book with its vagueness and its sometimes almost poetic idiocies, began to put on bulk.

Within days of settling in, three section members were sent out on detachment to Sorrento and the coastal towns, and Eric Williams, our best Italian speaker, became a solitary exile in the important town of Nola. Three more people, apart from the FSO, were tied down to administrative duties at HQ, leaving only four of us, Parkinson, Evans, Durham and myself, to confront the security problems of that anthill of humanity, the city of Naples itself.

First impressions of my colleagues under working conditions

28

are favourable. They are hampered in several cases by their lack of Italian, but they are an industrious lot, and set to work with enthusiasm to learn the language. Like all sections, this has developed its own personality. It is less informal than most, and a little bureaucratic. I cannot imagine any member of 312 FSS being able to manœuvre himself into a position where he could turn up at an airfield, wave his pass about, and bamboozle some Airforce officer, British or American, into arranging a quick unofficial flight back to England – an achievement of the kind which has been possible in certain other sections. All my new friends have been issued with special officer's-type identity documents replacing the normal AB 64, but Captain Cartwright has clearly not wished to have these endorsed as in the case of those issued to 91 FSS – one of which I still carry – with the authorization to be in any place, at any time, and in any dress. Nor, so far, do section members wear civilian clothes. Army Books No. 466 (no erasures, no pages to be detached) are scrupulously carried, and daily entries condensed in the form of a log, handed in to the FSO first thing each morning, and discussed at a parade at nine, at which certain regimental formalities are carefully preserved. These things are quite new in my experience.

October 8

Contact with the military units brought its inevitable consequences. The phone started ringing first thing in the morning and rarely stopped. An excited officer was usually on the line to report the presence in his area of an enemy agent, or a secret transmitter, or a suspected cache of abandoned German loot. All this information came from local civilians who poured into the nearest army HQ, anxious to unburden themselves of secrets of all kinds, but as not even phrase books had been issued to help with the language problem, mistakes were frequent. Today, being the only section member left in the office, I was sent hurriedly on the motor-bike, in response to the most urgent request, to Afragola, where an infantry major was convinced from local reports that a village woman was a spy. In this case evidence had been transmitted mostly by gestures which the Major had failed to interpret. It turned out that what the villagers had been trying to explain was that the woman was a witch, and that if allowed to cast her malefic gaze on the unit's water supply, she would make it undrinkable.

On my way to resolve this misunderstanding I saw a remarkable spectacle. Hundreds, possibly thousands of Italians, most of them women and children, were in the fields all along the roadside driven by their hunger to search for edible plants. I stopped to speak to a group of them, and they told me that they had left their homes in Naples at daybreak, and had had to walk for between two and three hours to reach the spot where I found them – seven or eight miles out of town. Here a fair number of plants could still be found, although nearer the city the fields had been stripped of everything that could be eaten. There were about fifteen different kinds of plants which were worth collecting, most of them bitter in flavour. All I recognized among their collections were dandelions. I saw other parties netting birds, and these had managed to catch a few sparrows and some tiny warblers which they said were common at this time of the year, attracted by the fruit in the orchards. They told me they had to face the hostility of the local people, on whose lands they were trespassing, and who accused them of raids on their vineyards and vegetable patches.

October 9

This afternoon, another trip along the sea-front at Santa Lucia provided a similar spectacle of the desperate hunt for food. Rocks were piled up here against the sea wall and innumerable children were at work among them. I learned that they were prising limpets off the rocks, all the winkles and sea-snails having been long since exhausted. A pint of limpets sold at the roadside fetched about two lire, and if boiled long enough could be expected to add some faint, fishy flavour to a broth produced from any edible odds and ends. Inexplicably, no boats were allowed out yet to fish. Nothing, absolutely nothing that can be tackled by the human digestive system is wasted in Naples. The butchers' shops that have opened here and there sell nothing wc would consider acceptable as meat, but their displays of scraps of offal are set out with art, and handled with reverence : chickens' heads – from which the beak has been neatly trimmed – cost five lire; a little grey pile of chickens' intestines in a brightly polished saucer, five lire; a gizzard, three lire; calves' trotters two lire apiece; a large piece of windpipe, seven lire. Little queues wait to be served with these delicacies. There is a persistent rumour of a decline in the cat population of the city.

October 10

How lucky for all concerned that the liberation of Naples happened when it did – when the fruit harvests were still to be gathered in – and the perfect weather of early autumn helped hardships of all kinds to be more endurable. Day followed day of unbroken sunshine, although the heat of summer had gone. From where I sat sifting wearily through the mountains of vilification and calumny, I could refresh myself by looking down into the narrow street running along one side of the palazzo. This is inhabited to bursting-point with working-class families, whose custom it is to live as much as they can of their lives out of doors, for which reason this street is as noisy as a tropical aviary.

Quite early in the morning, a family living in the house opposite carried out a table and stood it in the street close to their doorway. This was briskly covered with a green cloth with tassels. Chairs were placed round it at an exact distance apart and on it were stood several framed photographs, a vase of artificial flowers, a small cage containing a goldfinch, and several ornate little glasses, which were polished from time to time as the day passed by to remove the dust. Round this table the family lived in what was in fact a room without walls; a mother, grandfather and grandmother, a girl in her late teens, and two dynamic boys, who constantly came and went. Here the mother attended to the girl's hair, washed the boys' faces, served something from a steaming pot at mid-day, sewed and did the family washing in the afternoon. There were a number of other such tables along the street, and constant social migrations took place as neighbours paid each other visits. The scene was a placid one. The green *persianas* hanging over all the upper windows and balconies breathed in and out gently in the mild breeze from the sea. People called musically to each other over great distances. A beggar with tiny, twisted legs was carried out by his friends and propped up in a comfortable position against the wall, where he started to strum a mandolin. Two lean, hip-swinging American soldiers, sharing a bottle of wine, passed down the street, and the girl at the table looked up and followed them with her eyes until they turned the corner and disappeared from sight.

There is no notice in the palazzo to say who we are and what we are doing here so it is hard to understand why people assume this to be the headquarters of the British Secret Police. However, they do and we are beginning to receive a stream of visitors, all of them offering their services as informers. No question ever arises of payment. Our visitors are prepared to work for us out of pure and unalloyed devotion to the Allied cause. In the main they are drawn from the professional classes, and hand over beautifully engraved cards describing them as *Avvocato, Dottore, Ingeniere* or *Professore*. They are all most dignified, some impressive, and they talk in low, conspiratorial voices. We received a visit, too, from a priest with a pocketful of denunciations who asked for a permit to be allowed to carry a pistol. These are the often shabby and warped personalities on which we depend. Once they were called by their real names, now they are officially 'informants', and already there is a euphemistic tendency to turn them into 'contacts'. They are a special breed, the life's blood of Intelligence, and the world over they have an extraordinary thing in common: a strange and exclusive loyalty to one particular master. An informer is like a duckling newly freed from its shell and in need of fostering. He can be counted upon to attach himself permanently to the first person who is prepared to listen sympathetically to what he has to say, and prefers never to transfer his allegiance. In these first few days we all made half a dozen or so 'contacts'.

All names are checked as a matter of course with our rapidly expanding files, and we find to our amusement that several of these men who have come forward to assist us in every way they can, have been accused by their fellow citizens of being arch-collaborators. We have collected copies from the offices of the German Consulate of many servile and congratulatory letters written by Neapolitan worthies to Adolf Hitler himself. An outstanding example of these was from a Counsellor at the Naples Court of Appeal who had just called to offer his services. This assured the Führer of 'my great admiration and sympathy for the soldiers of your country', and concluded, *'Con profonde devota osservanza'*.

What is remarkable to us is the German bureaucratic rectitude with which all these communications, many of them highly nonsensical, have been conscientiously acknowledged, translated, and actually forwarded to the Chancery of the Nazi Party in Berlin, and fulsomely replied to by that office – the reply being returned via the German Embassy in Rome. One's imagination reels at the thought of the paperwork involved in dealing with thousands of such epistles from the toadies of occupied Europe.

Complaints are coming in about looting by Allied troops. The officers in this war have shown themselves to be much abler at this kind of thing than the other ranks. The charge has been made that officers of the King's Dragoon Guards, to whom fell the honour of being the first British unit to enter Naples, have cut the paintings from the frames in the Princess's Palace, and made off with the collection of Capodimonte china. The OSS have cleaned out Achille Lauro's sumptuous house. Some of the bulkier items of booty are stated to have been crated up for return to England with the connivance of the Navy.

October 13

A week in which our activities have been hampered, and even frustrated, by false alarms and scares of every conceivable kind. Anyone whose activities depart in any way from the standards of normality set by the city is regarded as a spy, and we have been involved in endless wild-goose chases. None of these forays out into the night produced results. The suspected spies were always harmless eccentrics. The mysterious stranger in the next flat tinkering with a powerful radio was not an enemy agent operating a transmitter, but a man trying to get the BBC. In houses said to contain caches of arms we found nothing more lethal than unemptied babies' chamber-pots; while flashing lights in the night were always people on their way to the cess-pit at the bottom of the garden.

Now that the mail is operating normally again, a horde of censors are busily slitting open letters to probe for hidden meaning among the trivia of family and business correspondence, and when in doubt they fall back on us. Unhappily many telephone conversations are being monitored, too, and the typed out 'intercepts' sent to us contain their fair share of absurdity. The prize example received so far was one solemnly headed 'Illegal use of telescope'. This referred to a passage in an overheard conversation between two lovers in which the girl had said, 'I can't see you today because my husband will be here, but I'll admire you, as ever, through love's telescope.'

No. 3 District adds to these burdens by bombarding us with addenda for the Black Book, which serves as the rag-bag for everybody's paranoia. In one case we had to make an entry for a suspect about which nothing is known but his possession of three teats on the left breast, while another was described as 'having the face of a hypocrite'.

All these things encourage the growth of disbelief, so that when a few days ago reports began to come in about mysterious knocking sounds coming from the depths of the earth, we were unimpressed. But when yesterday the Italian Pubblica Sicurezza Police – sceptics like ourselves – were on the phone to talk about the knockings, adding that they had even been heard by a senior policeman, notice had to be taken. The knockings had been reported from a number of widely separated areas in the northern part of the city. It was the police's theory, supported by much rumour and some credible evidence, that a picked squad of German SS had volunteered to remain behind after the German retreat from Naples, and that they had hidden in the catacombs, from which they might at any time make a surprise sortie. There was also a likelihood, if this were the case, that their plans had gone wrong, and that they had lost themselves in the darkness of a vast and only partially charted labyrinth, in which case the knocking could be explained as their attempt to draw attention to their predicament.

Only a small part of the catacombs – the most extensive in Italy, and possibly the world – is accessible to visitors and the police had had some difficulty in finding an old map showing their full extent. There was no way of knowing how accurate this map remained after the damage of the earth tremors of the past and the subsidences they were certain to have caused. However, the map was studied in its relation to the location of the places where knocking sounds had been heard and, the general opinion being that the Germans were down there somewhere, a force numbering about fifty men was assembled, to include the Italian Police, the American Counter-Intelligence

Corps and ourselves, to enter and explore the catacombs.

Of the two networks of catacombs under Naples, the principal one, which concerned us, is entered from the back of the church of San Gennaro. These catacombs are believed to date from the first century, and consist of four galleries, excavated one below the other, each gallery having numerous ramifications and lateral passages. The two nethermost galleries having partially fallen in, they have not been accessible in modern times.

It was decided to enter the catacombs shortly after dawn, and we arrived at the church in a dozen jeeps, lavishly equipped with gear of the kind used in cave-exploration, as well as all the usual weaponry. The monks in charge were already up and about, and showed us extreme hostility. One monk who planted himself, arms outstretched, at the entrance to the catacombs had to be removed by force, and then, when we went in, followed us, keeping up a resounding denunciation of our desecration of a holy place.

The Americans had equipped themselves with lamps like miniature searchlights; these shone on the walls of the anterooms through which we passed to reach the galleries, showing them to be so closely covered with frescoes – mostly in excellent condition after sixteen centuries – as to give the impression of colossal ikons. We were instantly confronted with the purpose for which the catacombs had been designed. Rows of niches forming burial chambers had been cut one above the other in the walls, and all these were crammed with skeletons, many said to have been plague victims of the sixteenth century. When somebody picked up a skull to examine it the angry monk trudging at our heels roared at him to put it back. Questioned about the possibility of Germans being in the catacombs, this man had answered in an evasive and suspicious way.

It soon became clear that we were looking for a needle in a haystack. We were in narrow, bone-choked streets, with innumerable side turnings to be explored, each with its many dark chambers in any one of which our quarry could have hidden, or from which they could have suddenly sprung out to ambush us, if they were still alive. These men, had they gone into the catacombs – and we were all still convinced they had – must have been in the darkness for nearly a fortnight since their torch batteries had finally given out. After which, groping their way, or crawling about among the bones, they would have encountered terrible hazards. Even in the second gallery we came suddenly to a black chasm. In the depths of this, where the whole roadway from wall to wall had caved in, the lights showed us a pile of dust from which protruded a few ancient rib-bones. We dangled a microphone into this pit and listened while the monk muttered at our backs, but the silence below was absolute.

We gave up and went back. It was two days now since the last knocking had been reported, and strange that the strength of men, however close to starvation, should have ebbed so suddenly that we could hear not even a moan or cry. The general opinion was that the monk knew more than he was prepared to say. There was even the possibility, the Police Commissario suggested, that he had gone into the catacombs and rescued the Germans. Whether or not this was so, it was unlikely that we should ever know.

October 15

Among the civilian contacts of these first few days, my prize acquisition was Vincente Lattarullo, a man steeped in the knowledge of the ways of Naples.

When originally asked what was his business with us, he answered in a dry whisper, 'I am motivated by a passion for justice,' and, saying this, he appeared to vibrate. It turned out that this distinguished, fragile-looking man, who sometimes halted in mid-sentence and swayed a little, as if about to faint, wished to denounce the activities of an American requisition-ing officer who was going round offering Italian car-owners a guarantee against their cars being requisitioned on payment of 100,000 lire. We told him that there was absolutely nothing we could do about it.

I took him to the Bar Vittoria next door for a *marsala all'uovo*, but when the barman brought the egg to be broken into his glass I saw the anguish in Lattarullo's face, and stopped him in mid-action. Apologies streamed forth and then Lattarullo begged to be allowed to take the egg home. Moments later the impact of the alcohol on an empty stomach set him swaying again and I realized that the man was starving. Unfortunately there was no food of any kind anywhere within range, except the prized and precious eggs, rationed on a basis of one per day to favoured customers. However, Lattarullo was prevailed upon to accept my egg as well, which he beat up in a cup, and swallowed very slowly there and then.

He proved to be one of the four thousand lawyers of Naples, ninety per cent of whom – surplus to the needs of the courts – had never practised, and who for the most part lived in extreme penury. There are estimated to be at least as many medical doctors in a similar situation; these famished professionals being the end-product of the determination of every middle-class Neapolitan family to have a uselessly qualified son. The parents are prepared to go hungry so long as the son is entitled to be addressed with respect as *avvocato*, or *dottore*.

Lattarullo had succeeded in staying alive on a legacy originally worth about a pound a week, now reduced by devaluation to about five shillings, and in order to do this had worked out a scientific system of self-restraints. He stayed most of the day in bed, and when he got up walked short distances along a planned itinerary, stopping to rest every few hundred yards in a church. He ate an evening meal only, normally composed of a little bread dipped in olive oil, into which was rubbed a tomato. Sometimes he visited another professional man in similar circumstances and they exchanged gossip, sipped a cup of coffee made from roasted acorns, and starved socially for an hour or so. He gave the impression that he knew everything that was going on in Naples. I walked back to his flat with him, and found him living in two rooms containing three chairs, a bed, and a rickety table on which stood an embittered aspidistra plant. The lighting and the water had been cut off years ago, he said.

It appeared that Lattarullo had a secondary profession producing occasional windfalls of revenue. This had to be suspended in the present emergency. He admitted with a touch of pride to acting as a *Zio di Roma* – an 'uncle from Rome' – at funerals. Neapolitan funerals are obsessed with face. A man who may have been a near-pauper all his life is certain to be put away in a magnificent coffin, but apart from that no other little touch likely to honour the dead and increase the bereaved family's prestige is overlooked.

The uncle from Rome is a popular character in this little farce. Why should people insist on Rome? Why not Bari or Taranto? But no, Rome it has to be. The uncle lets it be known that he has just arrived on the Rome express, or he shows up at the slum tenement or lowly *basso* in an Alfa-Romeo with a Roman number-plate and an SPQR badge, out of which he steps in his well-cut morning suit, on the jacket lapel of which he sports the ribbon of a Commendatore of the Crown of Italy, to temper with his restrained and dignified condolences the theatrical display of Neapolitan grief.

Lattarullo said that he had frequently played this part. His qualifications were his patrician appearance, and a studied Roman accent and manner. He never uses the third person singular personal pronoun *lui*, as all the people who surround him do, but says *egli*, as they do in text-books, and he addresses all and sundry with old-fashioned politeness as *lei*. Where the Neapolitans tend to familiarity and ingratiation, Lattarullo shows a proper Roman aloofness and taciturnity. When Lattarullo meets a man he says *buon giorno* and leaves it at that, and he goes off with a curt goodbye. This, say the Neapolitans,

who are fulsome and cloying in their greetings, is how a real
Roman gentleman speaks. If anybody at the wake happens
to have noticed Lattarullo about the streets of Naples on other
occasions, he takes care to keep it to himself.

October 20

A narrow escape today while motor-cycling along the Via
Partenope. I was riding towards the Castel Nuovo, through
an area badly damaged by bombing, with the sea on the right
and semi-derelict buildings on the left, when I noticed a
sudden change ahead from blue sky, sunshine and shadow,
to a great opaque whiteness, shutting off the view of the port.
The effect was one of a whole district blotted out by a pall
of the white smoke sometimes spread from the chimneys of
a factory producing lime. On turning a bend, I came upon
an apocalyptic scene. A number of buildings including a bank
had been pulverized by a terrific explosion that had clearly
just taken place. Bodies were scattered all over the street, but
here and there among them stood the living as motionless as
statues, and all coated in thick white dust. What engraved
this scene on the mind and the imagination was that nothing
moved, and that the silence was total. Dust drifted down from
the sky like a most delicate snowfall. A woman stood like Lot's
wife turned to salt beside a cart drawn by two mules. One
mule lay apparently dead, the other stood quietly at its side,
without so much as twitching an ear. Nearby two men lay in
the positions of bodies overcome by the ash at Pompeii, and
a third, who had probably been in their company, stood
swaying very slightly, his eyes shut. I spoke to him, but he
did not reply. There was no blood to be seen anywhere.

This turned out to be one of a series of explosions produced
by delayed-action explosive devices constructed by the Germans shortly before their departure, in each case from several
hundred mines buried under principal buildings. My friend
White's visit to the Central Post Office at about the time I was

motor-cycling along the Via Partenope nearly involved him
in disaster. He had gone there to discuss the reorganization of
the postal services and − I suspect − methods of censorship,
and about ten minutes after he left the building blew up,
killing heaven knows how many passers-by. A senseless
massacre perpetrated on the Italian civil population.

It now came out that several days before the Germans abandoned Naples, Colonel Scholl, the officer in command of the
garrison, reported to have been unable to accept Italians as
even honorary Aryans, had given an order that an area to a
depth of 300 metres from the sea-front be evacuated by the
civilian population. The Italians had been led to believe at
that time that a naval bombardment, followed by an Allied
landing, was expected in the city itself. The supposition now
was that the real motive was to clear the area to enable this
to be secretly mined, and that a large number of sea-front
buildings had been mined in this way, and might blow up at
any time.

Our most urgent preoccupation is the fact that our palazzo
may have been included, and this demoralizing possibility
strengthened to probability when our *portiere* told us that,
returning after four days' enforced absence with relations living
near the Porta Capuana, he had found a number of lengths
of wire strewn about the courtyard. The Engineers, who are
running round in circles trying to deal with this situation, will
go over the place as soon as they can, but their Captain,
contacted by the FSO, wasn't hopeful. The foundations of an
old palazzo like ours would be honeycombed, he said, with
sewers, cellars, and disused well-shafts. Even if there were
mines, the odds were ten to one they'd never be found. His
advice was to get out of the place for a few days, and wait
until buildings stopped blowing up.

This evening, after a day so full of alarms, the city was
plunged into even deeper misery by the first German air-raid.

Many bombs fell in the port area, and the nearest explosion caused our old palazzo to teeter hideously. As soon as the all-clear sounded I went out to inspect the damage, finding very little of consequence in the port itself but devastation in the narrow streets to the rear of it. Apocalyptic scenes as people clawed about in the ruins, some of them howling like dogs, in the hopeless attempt to rescue those trapped under the masonry. In Pizzo-Falcone a team of roadsweepers were working by lamplight clearing up what looked like a lake of spilled stew where a crowded shelter had received a direct hit.

October 22

There is no relief in sight to the near-famine conditions in the city and surrounding country.

Friday, at least ten jobs came up, among which was the visit to a peasant house near Aversa where the people had been assaulted by deserters. Having found nothing lootable, they had molested all the womenfolk, subjecting them to every conceivable indignity, including attempted buggery. The women were evidently spared from outright rape by the fear many of our soldiers share of contracting syphilis. One of the girls involved in this nightmarish business was outstandingly pretty, although spoiled by a puffiness – a sogginess of the flesh showing particularly about the eyes. This I've noticed so often in people close to starvation. I did my best to pacify the sufferers with vague promises of redress. There was nothing else to do.

Today the same girl appeared at HQ, eyes downcast, and shaking. She brought a letter from her father, which, from its unusual literacy, I suspected might have been put together by the village priest.

Sir,

I noticed when your honour was good enough to call that from the way you looked at my daughter she made a good impression on you.

This girl, as you know, has no mother, and she hasn't eaten for days. Being out of work I can't feed my family. If you could arrange to give her a good square meal once a day, I'd be quite happy for her to stay, and perhaps we could come to some mutually satisfactory understanding in due course.

Your humble servant.

October 23

A tremendous scare this morning following information given by a captured enemy agent that thousands of delayed-action mines would explode when the city's electricity supply was switched on. This was timed for 2 p.m. today. An order was given for the whole of Naples to be evacuated, and within minutes army vehicles were tearing up and down the streets broadcasting instructions to the civilian population.

The scene as the great exodus started, and a million and a half people left their houses and crowded into the streets, was like some Biblical calamity. Everyone had to be got away to the safety of the heights of the Vomero, Fontanelle and the Observatory, overlooking the town. This meant that the bed-ridden, the dying, and all the women in labour had to be coped with in some way or other, not to mention the physically and mentally sick persons in clinics all over the town. The agent had specifically mentioned that 5000 mines had been laid under the enormous building housing the 92nd General Hospital, packed at this time with war casualties, all of whom had to be moved to a place of safety. Our own move took place shortly before midday when streets were beginning to clear of the last of the desperate crowds. I saw men carrying their old parents on their backs, and at one moment a single, small explosion set off a panic with women and children running screaming in all directions, leaving trails of urine.

At the Vomero we took up positions at a spot on the heights where the road had been intentionally widened to assist visitors to appreciate the view, which was splendid indeed. All Naples lay spread out beneath us like an antique map, on which the artist had drawn with almost exaggerated care the many gardens, the castles, the towers and the cupolas. For the first time, awaiting the cataclysm, I appreciated the magnificence of this city, seen at a distance which cleansed it of its wartime tegument of grime, and for the first time I realized how un-European, how oriental it was. Nothing moved but a distant floating confetti of doves. A great silence had fallen and we looked down and awaited the moment of devastation. At about four o'clock the order came for everyone to go home.

October 24

The FSO called me in this morning to say that yesterday's great fiasco was the result of a carefully organized plot, designed to cause the maximum disruption to the life of the city. A young German soldier named Sauro had volunteered to stay behind when the troops pulled out and then, as soon as the mined buildings started to go up, to turn himself in with this story of the whole of the town having been mined. The General, exasperated, was of the opinion that this soldier should be treated as a spy, and shot. My instructions were to go to see him at the civilian prison at Poggio Reale and report on all the circumstances of the case, to help decide whether his execution could be legally justified.

Never having been in a prison before except the famous hole in the ground in Philippeville, into which dissident Arabs were flung, to be kept in total darkness, Poggio Reale came as a surprise. I stated my business at an office sited between the outer and inner walls – this was surrounded by weeping women – and a man appeared carrying an enormous bunch of keys, to walk with me to the inner gate. The man made some comment in Neapolitan dialect which I did not understand, and then burst out laughing. He gave me the impression of being insane. When we got to the gate he turned his back to it, and then, still giggling and chatting incomprehensibly, with his hands behind his back, selected the right key on the bunch purely by touch, thrust it unerringly into the lock and turned it. This was evidently a macabre piece of expertise to which all visitors such as myself were treated.

The gate opened; the screw, grinning with pride, waved me ahead and I stepped forward into the blue twilight of the prison, took its worn-out, fungus-smelling air into my lungs, and its resounding steel echoes into my ears. Next came the Ufficio Matricola, the records office, begrimed and gloomy – windows painted over against air-raid attacks – and staffed with unshaven, muttering clerks, looking hardly better off in their terrible version of freedom than the prisoners who dragged themselves about the place doing odd cleaning jobs. Here Sauro's whereabouts was established, and a warder with a face the colour of a newly unwrapped mummy took me to his cell.

I had expected a gigantic pale-eyed Teuton, but what I found was a small, dark boy who gave me a limp Hitler salute, and asked whether I'd brought any food. He said he'd had nothing to eat for two days. I found this believable at a time when the whole civilian population of Naples was still on the brink of starvation, and to the afflictions prisoners of Poggio Reale must normally have expected to suffer had been added the burden of an American master sergeant, attached as adviser to the office of the Warden, and engaged in the private sale of prison equipment.

Sauro told me that he was not a German at all but had had an Italian father and a German mother. His father had been killed at Tobruk, after which he had been taken to Germany by his grandparents, and there the rules had been bent a little in his favour to allow him to enter the Hitler Jugend. Although he was now seventeen years of age, he looked fifteen, with emaciated boyish good looks and fine dark eyes fixed with evident complacency on the vision of martyrdom. He had committed himself to this fate, and was prepared, virtuously, to avoid any compromise, or any kind of a deal that would help us to find an excuse not to shoot him. He preferred his death to be on our consciences, and refused to consider anything by way of an excuse that might have mitigated the severity of retribution. 'I did all the damage I could. I'm only sorry it couldn't have been more. Whatever I did was for the Führer. You can shoot me whenever you like.'

This was a dilemma. Much as generals may like to be thought capable of ruthless action, they often seem eager in practice to pass on moral responsibility for decisions of this kind. A Major Davis had been put in charge of this case and I sensed in the Major a reluctance to give the order for Sauro to be shot. I felt, too, although no positive lead was given, that the Section would not hold it against me if I found a loophole by which the firing squad could be avoided. This entirely suited my book, as I had no intention of being responsible for the death of a seventeen-year-old fanatic. I therefore reported that Sauro was mentally unbalanced. This verdict was accepted without comment, but probably with secret relief.

October 25

It is astonishing to witness the struggles of this city so shattered, so starved, so deprived of all those things that justify a city's existence, to adapt itself to a collapse into conditions which must resemble life in the Dark Ages. People camp out like Bedouins in deserts of brick. There is little food, little water, no salt, no soap. A lot of Neapolitans have lost their possessions, including most of their clothing, in the bombings, and I have seen some strange combinations of garments about the streets, including a man in an old dinner-jacket, knickerbockers and army boots, and several women in lacy confections that might have been made up from curtains. There are no cars but carts by the hundred, and a few antique coaches such as barouches and phaetons drawn by lean horses. Today at Posilippo I stopped to watch the methodical dismemberment of a stranded German half-track by a number of youths who were streaming away from it like leaf-cutter ants, carrying pieces of metal of all shapes and sizes. Fifty yards away a well-dressed lady with a feather in her hat squatted to milk a goat. At the water's edge below, two fishermen had roped together several doors salvaged from the ruins, piled their gear on these and were about to go fishing. Inexplicably no boats are allowed out, but nothing is said in the proclamation about rafts. Everyone improvises and adapts.

Tonight I dined for the first time in a civilian house at the invitation of a Signora Gentile recently released by a member of the section from the Filangieri gaol, where with a number of other women she had been imprisoned by the partisans on vague charges of collaboration. Here the mood was one of escapism, even of nostalgic frivolity. Our friends had made a huge effort to cast out of mind the unpleasantness of the immediate past. Several beautiful women were present – one in a blouse made from a Union Jack; all the old-style airs and graces banished by Mussolini were back again. The men kissed the ladies' hands, called each other 'egregious sir', and everybody used the polite form of address *lei* instead of the Fascists' forthright Roman *voi*.

We ate wurst, sipped schnapps, drank wine from glasses of the right shape and colour, somebody strummed a mandolin, and we talked about Naples and its traditions – the city that had ignored and finally overcome all its conquerors, dedicated entirely and everlastingly to the sweet things of life. Other wars were mentioned in passing, but this one was not. Neither were politics, Mussolini, food shortages or the rumoured outbreak of typhus.

All too soon the pleasant unreality of the evening was over, brought to an end by the curfew. As we were about to leave our hostess drew me aside and, showing a little hesitancy, said she had a favour to ask. She had a German soldier, she said, buried in her garden, and wondered what could be done about it. The story was that about two days before our arrival, when the partisans and the Germans were fighting on the streets, a German chased by armed Italians had knocked on the door and asked her to shelter him in the house. This she had felt unable to do, and next day, finding the soldier's body lying in the road outside, she had dragged it into the garden, taken a spade and buried it. What she was hoping now was that someone could be found to help in the task of digging this corpse up and smuggling it away, because it occurred to her that one day – perhaps even in years to come – she might want to sell the house, and she could imagine an embarrassing situation arising if the buyer happened to find a body in the garden. I told her that I could inform whatever authority it was that dealt with this kind of thing and leave it to them. She seemed disappointed, and said she wanted the thing done discreetly, and perhaps it would be better to leave things as they were. A mysterious business.

October 28

Neapolitans take their sex lives very seriously indeed. A woman called Lola, whom I met at the dinner-party given by Signora Gentile, arrived at HQ with some denunciation which went into the waste-paper basket as soon as her back was turned. She then asked if I could help her. It turned out she had taken a lover who is a captain in the RASC, but as he speaks no single word of Italian, communication can only be carried on by signs, and this gives rise to misunderstanding. Would I agree to interpret for them and settle certain basic matters?

Captain Frazer turned out to be a tall and handsome man some years Lola's junior. Having his hands on military supplies, he could keep her happy with unlimited quantities of our white bread, which for Neapolitans in general – who have been deprived of decent bread for two years – has come to symbolize all the luxury and the abundance of peace. She was also much impressed by his appearance. The Captain was a striking figure. His greatcoat had been specially made for him and it was the most handsome coat I had ever seen. His hat was pushed up in front and straightened with some kind of stiffener. This, although Frazer worked at a desk, made him look like an officer in a crack German SS formation. She wanted to know all about his marital status and he hers, and they lied to each other to their hearts' content while I kept a straight face and interpreted.

She asked me to mention to him in as tactful a way as possible that comment had been caused among her neighbours because he never called on her during the day. Conjugal visits at midday are *de rigueur* in Naples. This I explained, and Frazer promised to do better.

When the meeting was over we went off for a drink, and he confided to me that something was worrying him too. On inspecting her buttocks he had found them covered with hundreds of pinpoint marks, some clearly very small scars. What could they be? I put his mind at rest. These were the marks left by *iniezione reconstituenti*: injections which are given in many of the pharmacies of Naples and which many middle-class women receive daily to keep their sexual powers at their peak. Frequently the needle is not too clean, hence the scars.

She had made him understand by gestures one could only shudderingly imagine that her late husband – although half-starved, and even when in the early stages of tuberculosis from which he died – never failed to have intercourse with her less than six times a night. She also had a habit, which terrified Frazer, of keeping an eye on the bedside clock while he performed. I recommended him to drink – as the locals did – marsala with the yolks of eggs stirred into it, and to wear a medal of San Rocco, patron of *coitus reservatus*, which could be had in any religious-supplies shop.

This seemed the moment, as Lola had offered her services as an informant, to check on her background in the dossiers section on the top floor of the Questura. It appeared from her *fasciolo* that since the death of her husband she had been the

49

mistress of a Fascist hierarch, and there were sardonic references in typical police style to other episodes of her love-life. It seemed extraordinary to me that a Fascist leading light could do nothing to shield his private life from invasion by the police.

November 1

The miserable news is that Counter-Intelligence funds are to be reduced to 400 lire – £1 per week per section member. The meanness impelling this decision leaves us stunned. Most of us have up to a dozen contacts prepared to devote their time to our interests, and this wretched sum – paid in occupation money which costs nothing to print – is all that is available to compensate them. This announcement followed closely on the heels of the tidings that other ranks would be paid an extra 9s. per head to spend on Christmas festivities. What a peasant army this is!

Actually, although our paymasters have no way of knowing it, the money won't make any difference. The most dedicated informant, like the most devoted lover, rises above thoughts of monetary inducement to give what he has to give. What would make our task easier and give us a better conscience would be to offer these people who work for us, not money, but a little food. In large units – particularly American ones – it seems easy enough to smuggle rations out, and most soldiers who are invited into Italian homes find some way of taking the occasional tin of provisions with them. In a unit like ours of only thirteen men, rationing is absolutely cut and dried, and there are no extras to go astray. If anything happens to be left over at the end of a meal, our two servants see to it that no trace of it remains after they clear away. In this way, wherever we go, we go empty-handed.

Lattarullo called with a long whispered recital of new enormities on the part of the operators of the black market. He mentioned that the special Squadra Nucleo, organized by our vigilant Questore to act as a spearhead in the fight against corruption, had just been able to resolve a little problem for one of Naples's leading surgeons – who was already well known to us. It seemed that the doctor had managed to acquire a Fiat Mille Cinque-Cento, which turned out to have been stolen. In the ordinary way the regular Pubblica Sicurezza would have dealt with this predicament at a cost to the doctor of about 50,000 lire. As it is, he had the new Squadra to deal with, and has had to pay heavily for their incorruptibility – in fact 200,000 lire.

Lattarullo looked even weaker with hunger today than usual, and swayed from the waist, eyes closed, even when sitting down. After our chat I decided to take him for a meal to one of the side-street restaurants that have opened in the past few days.

We walked out together and faced this city which is literally tumbling about our ears. Everywhere there were piles of masonry, brought down by the air-raids, to be negotiated. Every few yards Lattarullo had to stop to gather breath and strength. When we tried to take a short cut through a familiar *vico* we found it freshly blocked by the collapse of tenements and filled with rubble to a depth of twenty feet. There was a terrible stench of shattered drains and possibly something worse, and the Middle Ages had returned to display all their deformities, their diseases, and their desperate trickeries. Hunchbacks are considered lucky, so they were everywhere, scuttling underfoot, and a buyer of the lottery tickets they offered for sale touched or stroked their humps as he made his purchase. A great collection of idiots and cretins included children propped against walls nodding their big heads. A legless little bundle had been balanced behind a saucer into which a few lire notes and a sweet had been thrown. In a matter of two hundred yards, I was approached three times by child-pimps, and Lattarullo, appropriately enough, was offered a cut-price coffin. The only food shops open were bakers, but they sold no bread – only sugary sweets: *torrone* and marzipan, all made with sugar stolen from the Allies, and fetching 30 lire for a tiny cube. We were stopped at a bottleneck caused by a collapsed building in the Vico Chiatamone where a sanitary post had been set up, and here every passer-by was sprayed with a white powder against the typhus.

We found the restaurant and took our seats among the middle-class patrons, who kept their overcoats on against the cold. All the coats were made from our stolen blankets. A choking deodorant disinfectant burning in a brazier set everybody coughing, but failed to cloak the smell of sewers seeping up through the flagstones.

The ritual in this restaurant is for a waiter to appear and pass through the tables carrying on a dish what Lattarullo calls 'the show-fish', for the customers to inspect with murmurs of admiration. This had a good-looking head, but the body had already been cut up in portions and was therefore unidentifiable. As usual, there was a trick in it. Lattarullo insisted on examining the fish and pointed out to me that the body didn't match the head, and from its triangular backbone evidently belonged to the dogfish family, which most people avoided eating if they could. The other recommended item on the menu was veal, Milanese style, very white but dry-looking, which the waiter, under pressure, admitted to being horse. We settled for macaroni.

No attempt was made to isolate the customers from the street. Ragged, hawk-eyed boys – the celebrated *scugnizzi* of Naples – wandered among the tables ready to dive on any crust that appeared to be overlooked, or to snatch up left-overs before they could be thrown to the cats. Once again I couldn't help noticing the intelligence – almost the intellectuality – of their expressions. No attempt was made to chase them away. They were simply treated as non-existent. The customers had withdrawn from the world while they communed with their food. An extraordinary cripple was dragged in, balancing face downwards on a trolley, only a few inches from the ground, arms and legs thrust out in spider fashion. Nobody took his eyes off his food for one second to glance down at him. This youth could not use his hands. One of the *scugnizzi* hunted down a piece of bread for him, turned his head sideways to stuff it between his teeth, and he was dragged out.

Suddenly five or six little girls between the ages of nine and twelve appeared in the doorway. They wore hideous straight black uniforms buttoned under their chins, and black boots and stockings, and their hair had been shorn short, prison-style. They were all weeping, and as they clung to each other and groped their way towards us, bumping into chairs and tables, I realized they were all blind. Tragedy and despair had been thrust upon us, and would not be shut out. I expected the indifferent diners to push back their plates, to get up and hold out their arms, but nobody moved. Forkfuls of food were thrust into open mouths, the rattle of conversation continued, nobody saw the tears.

Lattarullo explained that these little girls were from an orphanage on the Vomero, where he had heard – and he made a face – conditions were very bad. They had been brought down here, he found out, on a half-day's outing by an attendant who seemed unable or unwilling to stop them from being lured away by the smell of food.

The experience changed my outlook. Until now I had clung to the comforting belief that human beings eventually come to terms with pain and sorrow. Now I understood I was wrong, and like Paul I suffered a conversion – but to pessimism. These little girls, any one of whom could be my daughter, came into the restaurant weeping, and they were weeping when they were led away. I knew that, condemned to everlasting darkness, hunger and loss, they would weep on incessantly. They would never recover from their pain, and I would never recover from the memory of it.

November 5

Called for the first time on two new contacts, Ingeniere Losurdo and Avvocato Mosca, and found – no longer to my entire astonishment – that the circumstances of their lives bore an extreme resemblance to those of Lattarullo. Both lived in the Via Chiaia, once the resort of the town's aristocracy, in vast, dark, bare palazzi of which they occupied a single floor. Both palazzi date from the early eighteenth century, and have much-defaced coats of arms over the doorway. Each of them has its dim little porter's lodge, in which sits an identical old woman knitting in the semi-darkness, and a courtyard behind heavy doors with its flagstones rutted with the passage of the carriages of two centuries. There was a trace of embarrassment, a hint of apology, in the manner of both these men as they invited me into rooms which appeared to be virtually un-furnished. In each case I was led through a bare corridor to the *salotto*, in which a few pieces of furniture had been placed, without any attempt at arrangement, as if in an auction sale-room. They represented, I suspected, the whole contents of the apartment, hastily concentrated in a single room. The wallpaper – which in Naples had once signified pretension and luxury – was in both instances under attack by mould, and the paintwork on the doors and window-frames was cracked and flaking. A faintly vegetable odour noticeable in both palazzi suggested dry-rot. The general impression was one of genteel but very real poverty.

Ingeniere Losurdo and Avvocato Mosca were exactly fitted to their environment, for which reason they bore a striking resemblance to each other, and also to Lattarullo – so much so that they could easily have been members of the same family. I got the impression that they had been too poor to marry, too poor to do anything but defend themselves with considerable tenacity in the struggle to keep up appearances. They all offered an occasional, diffident reference to the fact that they were well-connected. Lattarullo's ancestor fought with Caracciolo in the war against Nelson and the Bourbons, and Mosca was entitled to put Conte on his visiting card, but no longer bothered. They had grand manners, and hearing them talk one sometimes seemed to be listening to Dr Johnson in an Italian translation. Each of these men had gracefully come to terms with a standard of living far lower than that of an average member of the Neapolitan working class.

In Naples one tends to blame all these things on the calamity of war, but after further acquaintance with the city, it becomes clear that this is only half the story and that the phenomenon of my three friends' near-destitution is an old and familiar one. The war has only aggravated their plight. In 1835 Alexander Dumas, who spent some weeks in Naples, wrote of its upper classes that only four families enjoyed great fortunes, that twenty were comfortably off, and the rest had to struggle to make ends meet. What mattered was to have a well-painted carriage harnessed up to a couple of old horses, a coachman in threadbare livery, and a private box at the San Carlo – where the social life of the town was largely conducted. People lived in their carriages or in the theatre, but their houses were barred to visitors, and hermetically sealed, as Dumas puts it, against foreigners like himself.

He discovered that all but a tiny handful of the ancient families of Naples lived in straitened circumstances, and this is roughly the situation a century later. They talked in a matter-of-fact and quite convincing way of the golden days of their families under Imperial Rome, but they had not enough to eat. The Neapolitan upper-crust of those times consumed only one meal every twenty-four hours; at two in the afternoon in winter, and at midnight in summer. Their food was almost as poor in quality and as monotonous as that served to prisoners in gaol : invariably the equivalent of a few pence' worth of macaroni flavoured with a little fish, and washed down with Asprino d'Aversa, tasting – according to Dumas – more like rough cider than wine. By way of an occasional extravagance one of these pauper-noblemen might force himself to go without bread or macaroni for a day, and spend what he had saved on an ice-cream to be eaten splendidly in public, at the fashionable Café Donzelli.

In those days the only profession open to a young man of good family was the diplomatic service, and as there were only sixty such posts offered by the Kingdom of Naples, the ninety per cent of applicants who were unsuccessful had to endure aristocratic idleness. The twentieth-century version of this situation as reflected in the somewhat sterile existences of Lattarullo, Losurdo and Mosca seemed little changed in its essentials. Nowadays the learned professions have taken the place of diplomacy, but they are so overcrowded they only provide a living for less than one man in ten who enters them. Lattarullo and company have been brought up to the idea that they cannot enter trade, and they are debarred by the same rule from physical creation of any kind. Therefore while others go hungry, they virtually starve.

November 10

The sexual attitudes of Neapolitans never fail to produce new surprises. Today Prince A., now well known to us all and an enthusiastic informant from our first days at the Riviera di Chiaia, visited us with his sister, whom we met for the first time. The Prince is the absentee landlord of a vast estate somewhere in the South, and owns a nearby palace stacked with family portraits and Chinese antiques. He is the head of what is regarded as the second or third noble family of Southern Italy. The Prince is about thirty years of age, and his sister could be twenty-four. Both are remarkably alike in appearance: thin, with extremely pale skin and cold, patrician expressions bordering on severity. The purpose of the visit was to enquire if we could arrange for the sister to enter an army brothel. We explained that there was no such institution in the British Army. 'A pity,' the Prince said. Both of them speak excellent English, learned from an English governess.

'Ah well, Luisa, I suppose if it can't be, it can't be.' They thanked us with polite calm, and departed.

Last week a section member was invited by a female contact to visit the Naples cemetery with her on the coming Sunday afternoon. Informants have to be cultivated in small ways whenever possible, and he was quite prepared to indulge a whim of this kind, in the belief that he would be escorting his friend on a visit to a family tomb, expecting to buy a bunch of chrysanthemums from the stall at the gate. However, hardly were they inside when the lady dragged him behind a tomb-stone, and then – despite the cold – lay down and pulled up her skirts. He noticed that the cemetery contained a number of other couples in vigorous activity in broad daylight. 'There were more people above ground than under it,' he said. It turned out that the cemetery is the lovers' lane of Naples, and custom is such that one becomes invisible as soon as one passes through the gates. If a visitor runs into anyone he knows neither a sign nor a glance can be exchanged, nor does one recognize any friend encountered on the 133 bus which goes to the cemetery. I have learned that to suggest to a lady a Sunday-afternoon ride on a 133 bus is tantamount to solicitation for immoral purposes.

In recognition of his medical interests in civilian life, Parkinson deals with the doctors of Naples. One of his most valuable contacts is Professore Placella, whose speciality is the restoration of virginity. He boasts that his replacement hymen is much better than the original, and that – costing only 10,000 lire – it takes the most vigorous husband up to three nights to demolish it.

November 15

Lattarullo invited me to lunch. I told him he couldn't afford it, and in any case where was the food to come from? He smiled mysteriously and said, 'You'll see.' He seemed so very eager for me to accept this invitation that I did so. Before going to his flat in the Via San Felice I ordered a couple of marsalas in our bar, and pocketed the eggs to take with me. I got to the flat and I found that another guest had arrived, introduced as Cavaliere Visco, a small man with enormously thick eyebrows, bad breath, and hands covered with hair. There was a faint, thin smell of cooking about the flat, as out of place as church incense in a brothel, and a neighbourhood girl who had obviously been called in to clean up was dragging herself about in the background with a mop. In Neapolitan fashion, Lattarullo had borrowed a chair here and crockery and cutlery there, and for this occasion his one remaining possession of value came into its own. This was a silver salver, stated to have been given to one of his ancestors by Vittorio Emanuele, which he had managed to hang on to through thick and thin.

The neighbourhood girl put her mop away, wiped her hands on her dress, went off, and came back shortly carrying the salver. I had seen this magnificent object with its embossed decoration of cupids and vine-leaves before, but only through the rents in the brown paper wrapper in which it was normally kept. Now, polished up and put to its proper use, I was dazzled by its splendour. As the girl carried the salver in, it seemed to draw all the light out of its surroundings, and Lattarullo and the Cavaliere became paler than ever, and Visco spread his hairy palms in delight.

The meal we were about to eat formed a tiny wet mound in the centre of the enormous dish, and I recognized it instantly from its odour, apart from its appearance, as 'Meat and Vegetables', the most disgusting of all Army rations. This little glutinous pile of age-old mutton was encircled by cubes of the dirty-grey bread of the kind sold on the black market. Visco whinnied with delight, and understanding the planning, the effort and the sacrifice that had gone into this offering, I managed a show of damp enthusiasm.

After the meal Lattarullo explained the reason for this meeting. He told me that he had become a member of a Separatist organization dedicated to the restoration of the Kingdom of the Two Sicilies, and that Visco was one of the leaders. Visco then set forth the philosophy and the aims of his movement. The South of Italy and Sicily, he argued, formed a cultural and economic unity, prosperous only when in political combination. Ruled from the North, these had always been written off as naturally backward areas, of value only as a source of cheap labour and cheap foodstuffs. I had to agree with this. The facts are, as every Italian will admit, that the South is virtually a colony of the industrialized North.

At this moment, Visco said, the South was faced with a new danger. With the collapse of Fascism, a political swing to the Left was certain. A high percentage of soldiers returning from the war were known to have been influenced by Communist ideas, and Visco and his friends believed that the North – traditionally the stronghold of Socialist sentiment – was destined to go Red. This being the case, he argued, the best hope for the South was to protect itself by cutting adrift from the rest of Italy, and re-forming the old political combination of Naples and Sicily either as a Christian anti-Socialist Monarchy leaning heavily for support on the West, or even as a colony of Great Britain, or as a new American State.

The way of life suggested for this new kingdom, colony or state seemed extraordinary. As industrialization lay, according to Visco, at the root of all social evil, it was to be rigorously suppressed, and the few factories already in existence in the South would be demolished. Southerners were to be returned to virtue on the soil. Field workers would be housed in barracks, clothed in knee-length homespun tunics in the style of the Roman peasants of old (the Patricians would wear togas), and fed on a low diet of maize gruel. They would be encouraged to early rising, early marriage, to regular prayer and the procreation of large families. Even the few existing tractors would be scrapped and replaced by the 'nail plough' in use in Roman times. Visco believed, too, in keeping women fully occupied. Whatever spare time was left over from their spinning was to be absorbed in profitable field-work, and they would labour at the side of the men, carrying their young babies as Indian squaws do, bound to their backs.

I listened gravely to these flights of fancy. Visco said that the Separatists had secret supporters everywhere, and that they would soon begin recruiting and drilling. Naturally they needed funds and arms. He hoped that the Allies would realize that any support they felt prepared to give to assist in the establishment of an anti-Communist state in an area of such vital strategic importance would be a wonderful investment.

Finally, he said, the Separatists would need experienced officers. He believed that the war with Germany would be over by Christmas, and with its ending the Separatists expected to open their offensive. Visco was prepared to offer me or any of my friends a commission in the Separatist army as soon as we were free from our present commitments. 'You could stay here when the war is over,' he said. 'Settle down and become a landowner . . . Here you would enjoy many privileges. You would live like a *barone*. Why go back to England and the fog?'

I listened with all the gravity I could manage, but found it hard to keep a straight face.

November 25

Food, for the Neapolitans, comes even before love, and its pursuit is equally insatiable and ingenious. They are almost as adaptable, too, as the Chinese in the matter of the food-stuffs they are prepared to consume. A contact from Nola mentioned that the villages in his area had lost all their breeding storks because last year the villagers eked out shortages by eating their nestlings. This is regarded as a calamity by those who did not benefit directly, as there is a widespread and superstitious aversion in Italy, as elsewhere, to molesting storks in any way.

Another example of culinary enterprise was provided by the consumption of all the tropical fish in Naples's celebrated aquarium in the days preceding the liberation, no fish being spared however strange and specialized in its appearance and habits. All Neapolitans believe that at the banquet offered to welcome General Mark Clark – who had expressed a preference for fish – the principal course was a baby manatee – the most prized item of the aquarium's collection – which was boiled and served with a garlic sauce. These two instances demonstrate a genius for improvisation. But some of the traditional local cooking is weird enough in its own right. On Vesuvius they make a soft cheese to which lamb's intestine is added. Shrove Tuesday's speciality is *sanguinaccio* – pig's blood cooked with chocolate and herbs.

My experience of Neapolitan gastronomy was expanded by an invitation to a dinner, the main feature of which was a spaghetti-eating competition. Such contests have been a normal feature of social life, latterly revived and raised almost to the level of a cult as a result of the reappearance on the black market of the necessary raw materials.

Present: men of gravity and substance, including an ex-Vice-Questore, a director of the Banco di Roma, and several leading lawyers – but no women. The portions of spaghetti were weighed out on a pair of scales before transfer to each plate. The method of attack was the classic one, said to have been introduced by Fernando IV, and demonstrated by him for the benefit of an ecstatic audience in his box at the Naples Opera. The forkful of spaghetti is lifted high into the air, and allowed to dangle and then drop into the open mouth, the head being held well back. I noticed that the most likely-looking contestants did not attempt to chew the spaghetti, but appeared to hold it in the throat which, when crammed, they emptied with a violent convulsion of the Adam's apple – sometimes going red in the face as they did so. Winner: a 65-year-old doctor who consumed four heaped platefuls weighing

1·4 kilograms, and was acclaimed by hand-clapping and cheers. These he cheerfully acknowledged and then left the room to vomit.

November 26

Most of the restaurants are open again, and these – though in theory out of bounds – are crowded with officers. Here the black market reigns supreme, and some of the prices asked, and obtained, are extraordinary. At Zi' Teresa's, a large lobster is said to cost up to the equivalent of a pound, and a good fish meal is priced at an exorbitant 10s. Wine is correspondingly expensive, with Chianti from a leading vineyard priced at 5s. a bottle. There is no need to pay these extravagant prices. All one has to do to have the restaurateur instantly and smilingly knock off half the charge is to ask him to sign the bill.

At Zi' Teresa's I ran into Captain Frazer, whom I had not seen for a couple of months. The change in his appearance was startling. I found him sitting alone engaged in the moody consumption of the raw semi-liquid custardy contents of a pile of bisected sea urchins, and it was clear he was not enjoying his meal. We had a confidential chat and he told me that he had been recommended to eat all the shellfish he could with a view to rectifying problems that had arisen in his relationship with the Signora Lola. In the shadows of the black market he could only afford sea urchins and found the whole business rather a chore. He appeared incredibly gaunt and wasted. His beautifully-cut uniform hung from his limbs, and when he got up and strode away, he looked more like a walking greatcoat than a living man.

December 5

The really unpleasant part about this job is having to make arrests. This is all the worse because we are convinced that these arrests are almost always unnecessary, and are the result

of manipulation by which we are dragged into private vendettas. This being so, there is a tendency when action of this
kind is in the offing to find some reason to stay away from
headquarters. Today, having overheard some mention of a
woman who would have to be picked up, I quietly slipped
away to Casoria, where I attended the funeral of a Carabiniere murdered yesterday by the bandits there (several professional wailers in attendance). The funeral over, I drank
a few marsalas with the Police Chief, went on to call on
contacts in the stricken town of Afragola, questioned a girl
of Madonna-like grace in Acerra who had most foolishly
applied to marry a guardsman at present serving six months
in the glass-house, and then meandered back to Naples. By this
time it was four in the afternoon, and I felt I was out of
danger. I was hardly in my room, beginning on my notes,
when Dashwood came in wearing his Buddhistic smile that
warned of calamity. 'Glad you're back,' he said. 'You're just
the man . . .'

The lady to be arrested and taken to the Filangieri prison
was a Signora Esposito-Lau, a German married to an Italian,
charged with nothing more serious than enthusiastic fraterniza-
tion with her countrymen in Naples, and with paying frequent
visits home to her parents in Frankfurt. In view of the Psychological Warfare Bureau's report (which I believe to be exaggerated) that 96 per cent of the Italian population collaborated
wholeheartedly with the Germans, it seemed absurd that this
woman, who had held no official position of any kind, and was
not known to have been a Nazi or a Fascist, should be singled
out for victimization, and I could only suppose that she or her
husband had made enemies who were avenging themselves in
this way.

My inexperience in these matters makes me awkward and
inept. The army provided no course, no instruction or advice
of any kind on how a woman should be arrested or how to
cope with the tempest of hysteria and grief when, without
warning of any kind, she is told that she is to be taken from

her home and her family and put in prison for an unspecified period. A small, frightened little Signor Esposito-Lau himself answered the door, with his wife at his heels. I mumbled what I had to say, and the wife fell to the ground in a faint, damaging her head on a chair. The neighbours on both sides had to be fetched to help resuscitate her, to console her, to dress her suitably for incarceration, and the house was soon full of weeping. I kept in the background, and found myself answering in an undertaker's whisper when anybody spoke to me.

Esposito-Lau, the husband, was quiet and dignified. He told me he was being punished for his success in business, and I'm sure he was. Unfortunately these people knew only too well the hunger and the freezing cold the frail-looking little wife would face in the Filangieri prison. There was a wild rush round to find articles of warm clothing, and when these were not forthcoming I calmed the crisis by telling them that I would come back next day, collect any missing articles and deliver them in person to the prison.

So I actually made some friends. One of the neighbours, a Signora Norah Gemelli, turned out to have an Irish mother and to speak perfect English. She made tea and we talked about Dante, and the unpleasantness of war, and gradually the sobs subsided and the tears were dried, and the fragile little prisoner hugged her husband and her friends for the last time, and made ready to go.

December 9

A day off on a remarkably fine Sunday for the season offered an opportunity for further acquaintance with the neighbourhood. Our surroundings provide a rare blend of grandeur and lower-class vivacity, the palaces among which we live having quite failed to keep the working man and his family at bay. From our front windows we look out over the formal gardens of the Villa Nazionale with their rare palms and their ranks of statues of the Greek heroes and gods, all of which have been contrived for the delight of the nobility of bygone generations, whereas the view from the office windows is straight into the 15-feet-high *portone* of the Calabritto Palace. Here, all the ground-floor rooms surrounding the vast court-yard, which is at once nursery, playground and market, have been taken over by small businesses : a clock-repairer, a maker of artificial flowers, a working cobbler, a tripe-boiler, a seam-stress, and others. In this way the many families who share the palace have developed their enclosed little village whose inhabitants hardly ever bother to leave it, since most of their requirements can be dealt with on the spot.

In my tour of the neighbourhood I found this social amalgam to be the normal thing; the poor and the rich in our *rione* live side by side, constantly rubbing elbows while appearing to be hardly conscious of each other's presence. Fifty or sixty per cent of poor families occupy one windowless room, and have been bred to endure airless nights on the ground floors of the palazzi, or in gloomy, sunless back streets. The aristocrats who remain make do with about twenty rooms on one of the upper floors of their ancestral home, and for the most part, let off the rest. In the past everybody who could afford to do so lived on the Riviera di Chiaia, where the sun and the sea air and the palm-shaded gardens defended them from the plagues and the poxes that constantly ravaged the labyrinthine city itself. Carraciolo, the hero of the Nea-politan republican insurrection, cold-bloodedly slaughtered by Nelson when our admiral intervened to put the effete Bourbon King back on the throne, lived a hundred yards away from our headquarters. I visited his family palace today, and found it the most charming of these great sea-front buildings, with a small courtyard with a fountain flanked by Roman busts, marble cherubs and prancing horses, the total effect being almost playful in the gravity of the Neapolitan-Catalan archi-tectural environment.

Exactly opposite the Palazzo Carraciolo in the Villa

Nazionale stands the now desolate aquarium in its grove of Judas trees and evergreen oaks, and I went there too. The Bay of Naples, said the sole remaining employee, was famous for its rare crustaceans and octopods, some of which were to be found nowhere else in the sea. They had had a unique collection of these, but they had all been fished out along with General Clark's unhappy manatee, to go into the pot in the first days of the liberation. A few molluscs and sea-anemones had survived for a matter of days, and then they, too, had died through the failure of the filtration plant.

The Via Carducci joins the Riviera at this point, and I followed it into the square containing the church of San Pasquale. This possesses the miraculously preserved body of the Blessed Egideo whom I found on view in the glass case in which he has lain for some two hundred years. The flesh, as proclaimed, showed no signs of decay, and the Blessed Egideo's facial expression was serene to the point of indifference. He enjoys huge fame in the area of San Pasquale as the protector of women in pregnancy, and only requires to add two more miracles to his already impressive list to complete all the qualifications for full sainthood.

San Pasquale is a community of its own, with its own fiestas and folklore, and even a surviving feudal chieftain, the Prince of Rocella, who raised a force of partisans in these streets and led them against the Germans in the celebrated four days of the uprising. Here I found myself immersed in the popular life of Naples which has been resurrected among the ruins. A hand-operated roundabout for children had been set up, and an old man with a concertina was squeaking out 'O Sole Mio' and selling printed fortunes for a lira apiece. Fishing has at last been legally resumed and in the street market an excited crowd had gathered to watch the cutting-up of a tremendous swordfish, rarely caught at this time of the year. The head had been cut off and stood up in the street for separate display, the sword pointing upwards and the huge flat blue eyes staring into the sky. This is a lucky sight, with phallic associations, and the onlookers circled the head reverently as if about to break into a dance.

Luck, and even more so bad luck, plays a powerful part in the lives of Neapolitans. There is not a jeweller's shop in the city that does not sell amulets in the form of a little coral horn to be worn on a necklace or a bracelet, and here in the Via Carducci something was pointed out to me which I did not imagine could exist – a house considered to suffer from the evil eye, which is carefully avoided by passers-by. There was nothing particularly sinister in the appearance of Number 15, which was just a small modern block of flats in which several tenants had put an end to their lives. The eventual remedy would be for a number of the neighbours to get together and put up the money to build a shrine in the street wall of the malefic building, placing it under the special protection of some powerful exorcist such as San Gaetano.

December 18

Again the vendetta. Not only are we subjected to a flood of accusations and denunciations that come direct from the Italian citizenry, but to a further, and usually even more sense-less and baseless outpouring, from the static military units in the area. These – road and railway construction companies, petrol supply companies, signal units, base depots, and so on – are thick on the ground in the Naples area, and their commanding officers soon fall victims to the Italian interpreters they employ who tell them what the interpreters think fit that they should know, and ply them with wild legends of spies and Fascist saboteurs. They also do what they can to involve these gullible and innocent men – just as they do us – in the local feuds.

The chiefs of police, being for the most part villains, figure very largely in these indignant reports from the units and recently a number of charges have been made against Marshal Benvenuto, who rules with a rod of iron in the village of

Torrito, near Aversa. An Italian police marshal is only the equivalent in rank of a sergeant-major, but he wields huge and often tyrannical power in small Italian towns, where he is in command of the forces of law and order. Benvenuto is said to use the unsatisfactory food situation to spread propaganda against the Allies, and in the words of one anonymous accusation 'to promise with open malice in a few days' time to arrest anybody who doesn't please him'. More seriously, he is charged with carrying on a personal vendetta against a famous partisan, Giovanni Albano, whom he arrested on an allegedly trumped-up charge soon after the Allies' arrival, and whom he has since been doing his best to have interned.

We really have too much on our plates to have to bother with this kind of thing, but the story of how we rewarded those who shed their blood for us in the 'heroic four days' of the partisan uprising at the end of September has to be prevented from becoming a legend, so today, with extreme reluctance, I took myself off to Torrito to see Albano and hear from him his story of what had happened.

Torrito seems to have had some pretensions to grandeur before falling into its present misery. All the houses in the main street had balconies. There was a small garden with a few palms in the little square, a school, a club, and three or four once-imposing mansions – now largely ruined. At the crossroads of the main street and the Aversa highway, on September 30, there took place a massacre conducted by the Germans. Twenty-four persons including a woman, a monk, and three boys in their teens, all the human beings the SS, who were in a hurry, could discover in the neighbouring houses, were lined up against the wall and shot. The massacre was a reprisal for the action of the partisans under Albano's leadership in the nearby village of Palo di Orta. I found the whole population of Torrito to be in mourning.

I was admitted with some caution to Albano's presence by a woman of his household, and found him a haggard, haunted man who spoke very quietly, as if in fear of being overheard.

His story of September 30 was that on that day the Germans were beginning their withdrawal from the area when a message reached Torrito that the Germans were at Palo di Orta, whereupon Albano and the twenty partisans he commanded had gone there to engage them. In the fighting which ensued, he and his partisans had captured two prisoners, six cars and a motor-cycle, and taken them back to Torrito. Here he sent for Marshal Benvenuto to demand his support in case of reprisals. But the Marshal ignored the summons. Albano then turned over the two German prisoners to the Marshal's safe-keeping, but Benvenuto, washing his hands of the whole enter-prise, not only released the two men but provided them with civilian clothes to lessen the likelihood of their recapture. Unfortunately, as it turned out, they were unable to find their way back to their unit. When the German tanks reached Torrito the two uniforms were discovered and, under the assumption the wearers had been killed, the massacre was ordered. Two days later, when the Allies arrived, Benvenuto arrested Albano on what sounded to me like the extraordinary charge of criminal collaboration with the Germans, and pro-duced several witnesses in support of these charges. He was sent to prison, and had been released on bail to await trial.

There seemed to be little material for an epic of the Resist-ance in this. Since Albano made no claim at any time to have actually killed Germans, it was to be supposed that he had not, and the two captured prisoners had been promptly released. On the other hand the charge of criminal collaboration seemed a strange one, so my first move was to visit the senior police officer for the area at Afragola, for a second opinion as to the true facts of the case. The marshall at Afragola was contemp-tuous of Albano's reputation as a folk-hero, describing him as a 'foreigner' from Sicily, and a member of the Sicilian Mafia. I then pressed for copies of statements made by witnesses in the case, and these were produced; one by a Luigi Pascarella, and another by a woman named Anna Consomata.

December 20

I checked Pascarella and Consomata in the dossier section of the Questura, and found that they both had records: Pascarella several times for pimping and petty theft, and Consomata for prostitution. After that both had to be visited. I found Pascarella at Fratta Maggiore, read his statement to him, and watched the changes in the small, mean, natural underdog's face.

'In August 1943 Giovanni Albano came to see me. He told me that two escaped Indian soldiers had taken shelter in his house. He said that he was worried because if they were found there he would be shot. I advised him to send them away but he said that he had heard that the Germans paid a reward for the recapture of escaped prisoners. He was very much against the Allies, and told me that if they won the war we should all be finished. I agreed to accompany him to the German Headquarters and there I heard him denounce the presence of the Indians in his house. Albano was known as an informer of the OVRA.'

'What was the actual date when Albano came to see you?' I asked him.

'It was the beginning of the month.'

'You were in prison until the 15th.'

'It could have been after that.'

'It wasn't. This statement is false. How did Marshal Benvenuto compel you to sign it?'

A moment of depressed silence, then a spread of hands as if to show the nail-marks in the palms. 'He threatened to frame my wife for prostitution if I didn't.'

Anna Consomata, at Caivano, was a beautiful girl, marvellously fair, an angel by Botticelli with tapering lute-playing fingers and coifs of yellow hair in the black South. To save time I mentioned her *fascicolo* in the Questura, and the conversation became frank. Sadly I learned that this golden

Venus had been the deplorable Pascarella's mistress and he had obliged her to back up his testimony by agreeing that she had been present on the occasion of Albano's visit. She had now established a relationship with the Commanding Officer of the local British Tipper Company.

After that it was Marshal Benvenuto's turn to be confronted with the evidence of his perfidy. We faced each other across his desk, the Marshal gaunt and grey, but defiant, seated under a padlocked showcase full of daggers taken from Torrito's desperados. A sawn-off shotgun leaned against the wall ready to hand. It seemed pointless to preach or to harangue in this atmosphere of siege. 'Why should you want to put Albano away?' I asked him.

'It had to be done,' he said. 'You've never lived here, so you don't understand the way things are. This is *Zona di Camorra* – gangster territory. We don't grow partisans in this particular soil. Albano wasn't interested in killing Germans. All he was out for was loot. I want to show you something to give you an idea of the trouble we're in after his famous action.'

He went off into the back of his office, returning with a brown rag which, held up and stretched out, was with some difficulty recognizable as a blood-stained shirt pierced by several holes. This, he explained, was the shirt worn by one of the men killed in the German reprisal. Twenty-one more such shirts remained in the possession of the families of the victims – the woman and the monk didn't come into this – and vendettas against Albano had been sworn on each of them. These bloody heirlooms would pass down to the family's eldest son in due course. In the absence of a son they had already been entrusted to the nearest male relative of the dead man. Albano, therefore, had twenty-one blood feuds on his hands; the shirt the Marshal had succeeded in confiscating belonged to a man with no family.

'This is the way things are done in Torrito,' the Marshal said. 'My personal inclination would have been to look in the other direction and let them get on with it, but the trouble is it wouldn't stop there. As soon as somebody killed Albano his people would take his shirt and divide it up between them and swear to keep the vendetta going. There'd be no end to the thing. What do you expect me to do? I have two men here. Half the town's starving. We have a dozen burglaries a night; hold-ups every day of the week; bandits all over the country-side. I haven't got the time or the strength to deal with a vendetta on top of all this. Somehow or other this man has to be got rid of.'

It was a problem one could sympathize with.

January 1

We have suffered from a plague of telephone-wire cutting, and there has been a case a day to deal with for the past week. Of all the miscellaneous jobs that are thrown at us, this is the most boring and frustrating. The most thankless, too, because we never produce results. In fact the only people so far to have caught wire-cutters are the Special Investigation Branch of the Military Police, and there have been bitter reflections at Army Headquarters on the subject of our comparative efficiency. The Army insists that these wire-cutting cases are deliberate acts of sabotage, whereas we know full well that lengths of cable are cut out purely for the commercial value of the copper, and that like any other article of Allied ownership the copper is offered openly for sale in the Via Forcella.

How is one supposed to begin to put a stop to this? All we can do is to visit the spot where the cutting has taken place and make enquiries – which are always pointless and profitless – from any Italians who happen to live in the neighbourhood. Last week my first on-the-spot investigation of this kind proved to be a perfect introduction to the conspiratorial silence of the South. About fifty yards of thick main cable had been cut, and at about seven in the evening right in the middle of the busy main street of Casoria. I went from house to house and shop to shop questioning people who in three cases out of four claimed to have had business compelling them to be in other parts of the town on the previous evening. Those who remained had seen or heard nothing. The *brigadiere* (sergeant) in charge of the Carabinieri station was not in the slightest surprised at this lack of success. *Omertà* – manliness, he explained. 'They side against us, and they always will do. It's a tradition.' I detected pride in his manner.

I reminded him that the Germans shot wire-cutters on the spot. 'Of course they did,' he agreed. 'Thank God, you're a civilized and humanitarian people, and you liberated us from those barbarians. You've taught us what democratic justice is all about and we can't thank you enough.' Not a muscle moved in his face to show that he was laughing at me.

Next day there was another case – at Cicciano. This time the man was actually caught red-handed by some British soldiers belonging to a local unit who happened to be passing, and who locked him up in their guardroom. The General, as generals do, wanted an execution. It looked an opportunity to instil terror into the hearts of those damned wogs who were tricking us right left and centre. I saw the prisoner, who looked sincere and produced his plausible story. *Of course* he had heard the noise of someone using a hatchet to chop into the wire, and *naturally* he had run out of his house to do what he could, whereupon the thieves had dropped the wire and dashed off. Our friend had felt it his duty as a responsible citizen to pick up the wire and throw it into his garden, where it would be out of harm's way, while he went off to report the incident to the police. At this point he was picked up.

Although this story was probably a typically Neapolitan cover-up, there was also a chance that it had happened in just this way, so I decided to give the man the benefit of the doubt and to do what I could to save his life. Once again there was a visit to the Carabinieri, and for a moment it was hard to believe that this wasn't the same *brigadiere* I'd seen the day before at Casoria. This man called me 'your honour' and within minutes found some excuse to congratulate me as the other had done for being the representative of a justice-loving country.

'Has the man a criminal record?' I asked.

'Your honour, his sheet's as clear as the soul of one of the innocents murdered by Herod.'

'I'm going to the Pubblica Sicurezza after I've done with you. If they give me a different story you're for it.'

'Your honour, I swear to you on the mourning worn for my sister who died a virgin – '

'Have you ever heard of *Omertà*?'

'I've heard of it, but surely you can't imagine it applies in my case? After all, we're both coppers. God knows, I'd sooner lie to my own father.'

The face remained a bland Neapolitan mask. I wrote, 'Carabinieri report no convictions,' and decided not even to bother to visit the PS, whose report was certain to be the same. What was one to expect? Why should these people sacrifice their countrymen to us any more than they had to the Germans? The verdict, so far as I was concerned, had to be insufficient evidence. If the General still wanted to go ahead with his firing squad, that was his responsibility.

January 5

I have been placed in charge of the security of a number of small towns to the north of Naples and within approximately 25 miles of the city; of these the largest are Casoria, Afragola, Acerra and Aversa. Although the Army certainly doesn't realize this, they are all located in the notorious Zona di Camorra. The task is a hopeless one, and it would be demoralizing to take it too seriously, but most of the last week has been spent in reconnoitring the area, and finding out what I can about these dismal places.

Seen from the outside through the orchards that surround them, all these towns look attractive enough : tiny versions of

Naples itself, clustered round their blue-domed churches. On the inside they are the showcases of poverty and misery. There are signs of a vanished prosperity. A few great houses have been built with arcaded fronts and a tower added here and there as an excuse for the rich landlords of the past to use up spare money, but they are falling into ruins, and squatters have built their shacks in the courtyards. The area is one of great natural fertility. It is from these orchards, fields and vineyards that the wealth was extracted to build the ducal palaces of Naples. A handful of families own all the land, and the peasants who work it have always done so in conditions that come very close to slavery. Nowadays the normal, accepted misery of their condition has been aggravated by the war and the loss of manpower. In some of these towns the whole population is said to be out of work. The new *sindacos*, the mayors who have been appointed by AMG, the Allied Military Government of Occupied Territory, to replace the old Fascist *podestàs*, are stated in the main to be members of the criminal Camorra. It is common knowledge that these have been appointed through the influence of Vito Genovese, the American gangster who, having obtained employment as an interpreter, has now manœuvred himself into a position of unassailable power in the military government. Law and order depend on badly equipped and badly armed Carabinieri and Pubblica Sicurezza, who have two or three men apiece in each town – all of them under constant threat of attack by well-armed criminals. When I called yesterday on the Carabinieri at Acerra, I was shown round the town by a *brigadiere* who walked at my side with pistol drawn and cocked. Last week bandits raided the police station here, killing the NCO on duty, wounding another policeman and taking the few poor obsolete weapons they had. This leaves only two Carabinieri to carry on.

In so far as anyone rules here at all, it is the Camorra. The Brigadiere gave the usual account of it as a secret and permanent resistance that had evolved over the centuries as a system of self-protection against the bullies and the tax-collectors of a succession of foreign governments who had installed themselves in Naples. The people of the Zona di Camorra lived by their own secret laws, recognized only their own secret courts, which imposed only one sentence on the enemy from without or the betrayer from within – death. In the old days, said the Brigadiere, there had been some sort of moral authority, some sort of justice, but now nothing but outright criminality remained. If there was plunder to be taken the Camorrista took it, and shared it out among his friends. The Camorristi were in big-scale organized crime, and they tolerated the police because they kept the small-time criminals in their place. The only man who had ever stood up to them had been Mussolini, who had sent thousands of troops into this area and thrown the Camorristi into gaol after farcical trials, or had simply sent them away for resettlement in other parts of Italy.

The police, here as elsewhere, are corrupt, and how can they be otherwise on the salaries they are expected to live on? The chief of police of every town – usually a strutting peacock of a man, uniformed like a general, although only an NCO, gets the equivalent, through the devaluation of the lira, of £3 a week. The Italian State has always encouraged its police force, by grossly underpaying them, to resort to the spoils system, and now with galloping inflation they are in effect receiving pay that buys between one-fifth and one-tenth of what it did before our arrival. My only incorruptible marshal is the old widower Lo Scalzo of Caivano, who is as grey and as starved-looking as my old friend Lattarullo, and whose appearance is a disgrace to the force. Having no family to worry about, he says, he can get by, or as he puts it – 'keep enough soup flowing'.

Discussing with Major Pecorella, CO of the Naples Carabinieri, this problem of corruption in the force, he put forward the rueful viewpoint that even a corrupt police force was better than no police at all. The main thing was to keep police rapacity within acceptable bounds. This interview was the result of many complaints from Resina, where it would appear that the Carabinieri have settled down to batten on the huge numbers of black-marketeers in the area. Last week they rounded up a band of *contrabandisti* and then freed them on payment of 15,000 lire per head. Another less affluent band got off with a total payment of 30,000 lire. The crunch came when they 'requisitioned' a lorry-load of leather belonging to the Consiglio di Economia, and held it at their barracks until a ransom of 20,000 lire was paid. Pecorella agreed that this was scandalous. Yet what was to be done? If he sacked the men they couldn't be replaced, and his force is only one-quarter of its regular strength.

The fact is that with all their shortcomings, the police manage to keep the walking corpse of law and order alive and on its feet, and some get themselves killed doing so. They tolerate the big racketeers of the Camorra because there is nothing they can do about them, and they gratefully accept whatever they are given in the way of protection money, but they are relentless in the war they wage on petty thieves, and for this, at least, the public is grateful.

January 7

Today I made my first contact in the Zona di Camorra, outside the police, when Lo Scalzo took me up to see Donna Maria Fidora, otherwise known as La Pitonessa (the Pythoness), who lives on her estate near Caivano, and is the richest landowner in this locality. Donna Maria was originally a circus performer who specialized in wrestling with a python, and in this way attracted the fascinated attention of Don Francisco Fidora, an intellectual who was writing a book on the circus, and who immediately proposed marriage and was accepted. A man twenty years her senior, and of delicate constitution, he was said by Lo Scalzo to have died of a heart attack either in the act of the marriage's consummation, or shortly after.

All this happened a decade ago, since which time the Marshal said Donna Maria had run the estate with professional efficiency. I found her a soft, well-rounded woman with a dreaming smile, no longer showing any signs of what must have been the impressive musculature of her youth. We drank fizzy wine from the estate, chewed on hard biscuits, and complained of the times we lived in. Later Lo Scalzo mentioned that Donna Maria employed her own private army to keep order on her land, for which reason it was an oasis of discipline and calm in the general anarchy of its environment. No one could pull the wool over her eyes, he said. She knew just as much about what went on behind the scenes as did the Sindaco himself, but – as the Camorra did not admit women to its membership – she was a far more dependable source of information from my point of view.

January 12

The epidemic of wire-cutting continues with the General's threats rumbling in the background and a great drive by the MPs. As usual the small people who cut the wire bear the brunt of the offensive, but no attempt is made to track down the traders who buy and sell the copper.

There is plenty of muddle and tragedy in this tiny corner of our war effort. Yesterday Antonio Priore, scrap-merchant, age unknown but thought to be about 70, was pushing his hand-cart through the streets of Afragola when he was stopped by an MP patrol who went through his load of scrap and found severed lengths of wire. Priore seemed at first to be under the impression that they were interested in buying the wire, and explained through the interpreter that there was plenty more where that came from. He was astonished to be arrested, contending that the wire was German; he claimed that Italians had been urged in Allied broadcasts during the German occupation to do just what he had done.

This was clearly the MP's pigeon, but for some reason I was dragged in and sent to see Priore in Poggio Reale, where I found him shivering and shaking in his cell. He was very old and decrepit, and if not positively half-witted, certainly far from bright. The old man was clearly bewildered to be in Poggio-Reale. He had always understood, he said, that the Allies had promised to reward Italians like himself who worked for their cause, and what better proof was there of the patriotic work he had undertaken than the possession of quantities of German wire? So far there had been no talk of rewarding him in any way, and all the thanks he had received was to be hauled off and thrown into prison. 'So the Allies won, eh? And good luck to them,' he said. 'I certainly did what little I could.' He clearly thought I had come to take him out. 'Be nice to get back home to the old woman,' he said. 'I didn't like to think of her in that house all on her own last night. Can't get about too well any more.' He had old, red, runny eyes that looked as though they were full of tears when I arrived, so it was difficult to decide whether or not he was weeping when I left.

In the afternoon I drove out to Afragola through cold, pitiless rain, and had great difficulty in finding the Priore shack in the waterlogged fields. Inside, hideous, stinking poverty; an old lady shrivelled as a mummy lying fully dressed under a pile of rags in a bed. Starving cats, rats, leaking roof, a suffocating smell of excrement. Not the slightest sign of food anywhere. Nearest house two hundred yards away.

At the Carabinieri Station I found the Brigadiere in a state of shock, sitting at his desk staring into space. He was suffering from daily gunfights between rival gangs, bandits, pillaging army deserters, vendettas, kidnappings, mysterious disappearances, reported cases of typhus, the non-arrival of his pay and the shortage of supplies of every kind, including ammunition, and it flabbergasted him that it was possible for anyone to be concerned about the fate of one abandoned old woman. 'If it worries you so much,' he said, 'why not just let the old man go?'

From Afragola I went to the MP's HQ to take away samples of wire, and then on to Signals for expert examination. 'Of course it's German wire,' the Captain said, 'but half the wire we use *is*. It's our wire now. Surely it all depends when the cutting took place?' He studied the copper where it had been chopped into. 'Looks quite bright, doesn't it?'

Back at HQ I recommended Priore's release, and was told that the recommendation was out of order. Priore was held in Poggio Reale at the disposition of the Military Police, noted for their stubborn defence of their territorial rights. So Priore would be brought to trial in a week's time – or maybe two weeks, or even three weeks, depending on pressure of business in the courts. Meanwhile the wife would die alone in their shack. There was nothing whatever to be done.

January 14

Rumours are the standby – the bread and butter – of any security section, and in a section like this where a daily report is insisted upon, and material has to be raked up to fill it from one source or another, they are avidly snatched up for use as space-fillers. It is said that in some sections, less worthy than ours, they are unscrupulously manufactured by section members themselves. At all events, whether true or – as in most cases – false, they are rarely of the slightest importance.

This morning's rumour, picked from my report by the FSO, proved to be the rare exception, and in reading it he fairly bounded from his chair and within minutes was on his way to Army Headquarters. The rumour was that an invasion was planned at Anzio, just south of Rome, and would take place next week. An hour or two later the FSO was back, frothing with excitement. In this case the rumour was fact. The invasion was on, and I was ordered forthwith to track down the source of the leak which might necessitate having to call the whole operation off.

A ticklish business indeed, because the information came from the Gemellis with whom I dined last night. Since the time of the arrest of their next-door neighbour Signora Esposito-Lau, I had struck up a friendship with both Norah and her husband Alberto, and it was a friendship of the kind that I hoped would outlast the war. Whenever I found myself at a loose end of an evening it had become my habit to run up to the Via Filippo Palizzi and spend it with my friends chatting about life in general, or listening to readings of poetry by Norah, usually from Dante or Leopardi. Through the Gemellis I had made a network of friendships, and now being told that I was obliged to go back to these people and browbeat them if necessary, to obtain further information, meant the certain loss of their confidence and their affection.

I saw Norah and did the best I could to explain the predicament I was in. The fact that she was only half Italian and had either inherited or believed she had inherited emotional attitudes from her Irish mother, clearly helped. She clung to a sentimental fictional view of our basic rectitude as a nation. I was Welsh, too, which was half way to being Irish. We were all Celts together, united in our little Camorra against the big Camorra of Naples, the Americans and other foreigners in general. The upshot was I got the name of an Ingeniere Crespi, at whose house at a dinner-party attended by the Gemellis the thing had started, and Norah went off to see Signora Crespi and prepare her for my visit.

Fortunately the honoured and terrible tradition of Omertà is gradually dying out in the Neapolitan upper classes. Had the sweet and smiling little Signora Crespi and her family inhabited a *basso* in Sant' Antonio Abate, stronghold in Naples of all the ancient and mysterious traditions, one of which raises the guest to the dignity and sanctity of a member of a family, she would not have talked. She would have ducked and dodged, and in

81

the end produced the inevitable trump card : 'I made it all up, I was lying to impress my friends, so do what you like about it.' But Signora Crespi lived in a Via dei Mille block of flats with a uniformed porter, and a lift that would work again one day, and her husband was a successful man and her son went to the university, and all these things had had their civilizing and their taming effect. The Signora talked, describing the occasion at another dinner-party when a British civilian technician employed by the Navy had become a little tipsy and boastful, reacting to the general contention that the war had reached a state of stalemate by brandishing the news of the impending invasion.

This was a textbook case of a breach of security, of the kind described at the Matlock course. One had heard of this kind of thing, but never believed that it could really happen. The fateful news of the landing might as well have been shouted by heralds down from the heights of the Vomero. It would have spread by now in all directions. If I had picked it up it was hard to believe that one of the line-crossers would not have done so too. It was clear from the FSO's alarm that all the terrific paraphernalia of preparation for an operation of this scale was well under way. The question was, dared we go ahead, with in all probability a fifty-fifty chance that the Germans would be dug in, waiting for us?

January 19

Another morning of terrible confusion in the Castel Capuano, with justice dispensed in the present eccentric, almost whimsical fashion. My interest was in the poor, half-witted old Antonio Priore, who had been arrested for cutting a main telephone cable to sell the copper. He didn't show up, so presumably – as is so often the case – he had got himself lost in the over-crowded gaol. While kicking my heels I looked in on a few other trials.

Most of these were farcical. The court was in the centre of

the Porta Capuana black-market district in which stolen army supplies of every kind were openly and abundantly displayed on every roadside stall, and yet there were men here in the dock laden with chains, to receive the current prison sentence of three months, plus a fine of 30,000 lire, for being found in possession of five or six cartons of American cigarettes. A case came up of a man charged with possession. An MP appeared and claimed to have arrested him, but the man, who had already been in prison six weeks, denied this. He told the judge he was arrested by a squad of MPs, not including this one, and had never been able to find out why. The MP gave his evidence in such a shaky manner that the judge repeatedly questioned him.

JUDGE : But do you remember him or don't you?

MP : There's something familiar about his face. That's all I can say. I've had fifty other cases since this man was picked up.

JUDGE : I wish to see your notes on this particular case.

It turned out that the MP had no notes, and the case was dismissed.

The man who had the good luck to be called immediately after this particular fiasco benefited from the young judge's increasing demoralization and got off with a fine of only 200 lire for possession of Army boots. There followed two far more serious cases in which not only did the witness for the prosecution fail to appear, but all the statements, which should have been attached to the other documents, were missing. The judge ordered the witnesses to be fetched immediately, but it was then discovered that instead of their home addresses, the only addresses given had been c/o the Central Police Station.

This might have been no more than another innocent example of chaos, or something more sinister – the bribery of prison or court officials in the hope that the judge would throw up his hands in despair and dismiss the case. If so, it could be a dangerous game for the defendants, because in this instance the judge ordered a postponement, and sentences were getting heavier every week.

The next man in the dock, charged with the possession of articles of military clothing, was a typical old Neapolitan sweat of the kind that pretends to be half-witted to be allowed to get away with his jokes. He was thoroughly enjoying himself, spoke in an exaggerated dialect hardly recognizable as Italian, and went in for a mime that sent up titters all over the court. The interpreter took care to leave out most of his asides, but the judge, bewildered and irritated by the laughter, wanted to know what it was all about.

JUDGE: Didn't he just say something about the Americans? What did he say?

INTERPRETER: Just a stupid remark, your honour. Nothing to do with the case.

JUDGE: Will you please leave it to me to decide what has to do with the case, and what has not. I insist on knowing what he said.

INTERPRETER: He said, 'When the Germans were here we ate once a day. Now the Americans have come we eat once a week.'

JUDGE: Ask him if it means nothing to him that we have freed him and his kind from Fascism. How can he talk about us and the Germans in the same breath?

The interpreter translated the judge's remarks and the old man rolled up his eyes, let out a derisive gabble, and then went through the gesture of displaying his sexual parts. A gale of laughter went up.

JUDGE: I'm losing all patience with him. What does he say now?

INTERPRETER: With respect, your honour, he says, Americans or Germans, it's all the same to him. We've been screwed by both of them.

JUDGE: He's off his head. Get him out of my sight. Case dismissed.

THE PRISONER: Best wishes, your lordship. May all your kids be males.

January 22

The Anzio landing took place yesterday, so far – miraculously – with every sign of success. It seems incredible the Germans should not have been ready and waiting. They must be asleep. On January 19, 35 maps of operational significance – presumably concerned with the landing – were found on the floor of a warehouse in Torre Annunziata. Civilians were taking them away to make a fire. They said that about 500 more had already been burned.

February 5

Thieves have scaled the ramparts of Castellammare castle, which houses the Field Security Headquarters for Italy, removed the wheels from all the vehicles, and escaped back with them over the walls, which are 30 feet in height. Despite sentries at the gate and roving patrols within, Castellammare – source of all discipline and doctrine in matters of security – has been breached and ravished. As the Italians put it, we've been *fottuti*. They see us as only one degree better than cuckolds. The operation, carried out with contemptuous ease, took about five minutes to complete. This will provide splendid material for the ballad-singers of the area, whose audiences revel in colourful villainy.

I was reminded by this display of audacity and resourcefulness of the first days of our arrival in Naples, and my amazement at the spectacle of a damaged tank abandoned at the Porta Capuana, which, although one never saw a finger laid on it, shrank away day by day, as if its armour-plating had been made of ice, until nothing whatever remained. Things have come a long way since then. There have been newspaper accounts of urban buses seen careering away into the remote fastness of the Apennines, there to be reduced in comfort to their component parts. Trams, left where they had come to a standstill when the departing Germans wrecked the generating station, have been spirited away in the night. A railway engine, stranded in open country owing to the looting of rails and sleepers, was driven off when these rails and sleepers were quite incredibly relaid, to a place more discreetly located for its demolition.

No feat, according to the newspapers and to public rumour, both of which dwell with great delight on such flamboyant acts of piracy, is too outrageous for this new breed of robber. In the region of Agropoli small ships left unguarded have been lifted out of the water and mysteriously transported away, and portions of their superstructures have later been discovered miles inland, hidden in orchards as if they had been carried there and left high and dry by some tidal wave. In revenge, said the newspaper reporting this case, a party of fishermen raided an isolated castle in the area and went off with tapestries which they used to repair their sails

Nothing has been too large or too small – from telegraph poles to phials of penicillin – to escape the Neapolitan klepto-mania. A week or two ago an orchestra playing at the San Carlo to an audience largely clothed in Allied hospital blankets, returned from a five-minute interval to find all its instruments missing. A theoretically priceless collection of Roman cameos was abstracted from the museum and replaced by modern imitations, the thief only learning – so the reports go – when he came to dispose of his booty that the originals themselves were counterfeit. Now the statues are disappearing from the public squares, and one cemetery has lost most of its tomb-stones. Even the manhole covers have been found to have a marketable value, so that suddenly these too have all gone, and everywhere there are holes in the road.

February 12

I have come to the conclusion that the people of Naples know nothing – and care nothing – for the life of the countryside around them. They have crowded together in their human rookeries to live the affable, rootless life of the soft city, having shed, probably with gratitude and relief, the uncomfortable traditions of the Italian South. When, for example, I talked to Lattarullo about such things as vendettas he replied intelligently and after some thought, but all he had to say might have been taken from a book dealing with primitive tribal customs. He had no first-hand knowledge at all of such things – nor had any of my Italian friends. Ten miles from the cafés of the Piazza Dante finds one deep in vendetta country – but Afragola with its Bronze-Age rituals might, for the Neapolitans, be a thousand miles away. The main road to Caserta, which everybody visited for its palace, passed through the outskirts of Afragola, but Lattarullo had never bothered to turn aside and drive a hundred yards or so into the town which gave both Al Capone and the Neapolitan clowns to the world – although he and all my other contacts had been to Rome many times. Afragola, which belonged to another age, and another world, was just as alien and incomprehensible to them as it was to me.

The numerous newspapers, too, are bored with rural topics, and the only time when these forgotten areas get a mention is when they are visited by some politician. Marshal Greco of Afragola mentioned some time ago that a 13-year-old boy recently waited in ambush and shot the man who had killed his father several months before he was born. An episode such as this, which seemed dramatic enough to me, was considered not worthy of mention in a local newspaper. When a man is killed here in the course of a vendetta (normally by a blast from a sawn-off shotgun), his mother if still alive will kiss and suck at his wounds in the presence of those invited to the funeral as a demonstration of her insatiable desire for vengeance. Greco or Lo Scalzo told me things like this, otherwise I would not know.

These reflections on the bloody dramas of the countryside that receive no publicity were provoked as a result of another visit to Poggio Reale to deliver a prisoner. I seemed to be treated by the grey little, scuttling, giggling men who run the administrative side of the prison as a member of the family, and they made every effort to keep me hanging about in the blue twilight of the office where I could be subjected to their macabre jokes while they pretended to look for lost documents or forms that had to be signed.

In this case, the prisoner had offered himself for employment by an Allied Military unit, and his name had been found to be on the Black List, hence his arrest. He claimed – quite possibly rightly, as this kind of thing often happened – that he had been arrested after being mistaken for a dangerous Fascist of the same name, that this was the third time it had happened, and that he'd just been released after serving three months before the mistake was discovered. It could happen, I agreed with him. People's names got on the Black List for all sorts of reasons, most of them absurd, and once a name was on the list it seemed impossible to remove it. I could only sympathize with him and promise to report his complaint. My own view was that half the prison population should never have been inside, and were there through the breakdown of justice.

As usual there was a long wait in the *Ufficio Matricola*, where prisoners go through all the ceremonies of admission or discharge. A man ahead of us, brought in by the American Counter-Intelligence Corps, was being fingerprinted, and one realized, even in such a small detail as this, how barbarous the system is, and how clear was the intention that the prisoner must be made to realize that everything civilized has been left behind. One of the office staff simply grabbed the man's hand, pressed the splayed-out fingers on to the inked pad, then on a form, and then gestured to him to go and wipe his fingers on the wall. Thousands of others had done this before him, so that coming into the office for the first time one had the impression that it had actually been painted in dark greens and blacks to represent the undergrowth and the trailing lianas of a tropical forest.

While my man was waiting his turn, four tiny men in prison uniform were led into the office chained together. I went over to them, and as their hands were manacled, stuck a cigarette in each mouth, lighted it, and asked them what they were doing there.

They explained that they were *ergastolani* – lifers, and that having completed their first year in solitary confinement, they were being taken to the island of Procida to complete their sentences.

'What are you in for?' I asked the first little man.

'Multiple homicide.'

'You don't look capable of it,' I said. The man in fact seemed the embodiment of harmlessness, with a face devoid of any of the obsessions that drive to murder. 'How many did you kill?'

'Three. My friend here killed five.'

The friend, jangling his chains, was pushed forward – a prize exhibit. He was the smallest of the four, and the meekest-looking. He was so ordinary, so mild, so free of any obvious psychopathic taint.

'How could you?' I asked him, but he took the question to mean 'how did you?' and gave me the gory details with great simplicity.

'I wiped out a whole family with a hatchet. It took five minutes. It was a quick, clean job. Nobody suffered. I did it for honour.'

The others agreed, they'd all killed for the same reason.

'Would you do it again?' I asked them.

'In the same circumstances we'd have to. It stands to reason. Don't imagine anybody enjoys having to do a thing like this. The fact is it was a mistake to get ourselves born.'

I gave them the rest of my cigarettes, and a few minutes later they were led away.

Antonio Priore was tried today and sentenced to three years

in prison. The full story of this appalling miscarriage of justice is that had he been sent to the court on the first day for which his trial was fixed, he would have been fined – as all wire-cutters were at that time. As he couldn't be found in the prison, the case was adjourned for seven days, by which time fines had been given up, and prison sentences of up to six months were the rule. Once again Priore was overlooked in the prison, and the case was further adjourned until today, when three years has become the minimum sentence for wire-cutting offences.

The MPs remained unmoved when I approached them to ask whether nothing could be done. I was told to mind my own business.

To Pomigliano today to arrest Cesare Rossi, once Mussolini's Press Secretary, accused of having been involved in the murder of Matteotti, the Socialist deputy who did all he could to prevent Mussolini from coming to power. This seems to be another case where we are being used as the catspaws of Italian political vendettas that have nothing whatever to do with us or the war effort.

I found Rossi at the barber's in the process of being shaved, and told him that history had finally caught up with him. He got up from the chair instantly and without demur, the barber wiped the lather from his face, and Rossi paid and tipped him, and away we went. He appeared a sombre and taciturn man. I found that he lived alone with his wife, and it was evident from the seediness of the surroundings and an odour of respectable poverty, that although he had been a founder member of Mussolini's Fascists, and at one point was even in the running for leadership, he had made very little out of it. I told him that he could have an hour to get his things together and say goodbye to his wife and neighbours, but he waved the offer away. The leave-taking occupied five minutes. He hugged his wife, kissed her on both cheeks, stuffed a few possessions into a small bag, and said, 'Let's go.' As we got into the car he called back, '*State boa*,' with a final wave. He was one of the most dignified men I had ever met, with inner reserves that enabled him to face calamity of this kind without the slightest outward sign of distress.

The drive back to Naples took a good hour, and after an interval of silence we talked a little. Rossi had no hesitation in telling me about the Matteotti affair, the international scandal which first displayed the violence and the potential ruthlessness of the Fascists to the world. Rossi's story was that the Sinclair Oil Company had paid a bribe of one million dollars to the deputy Finzi, a front for Mussolini, for the concession to carry out oil exploration, and that Matteotti had obtained proofs of this and had announced that he proposed to produce these proofs in the Chamber of Deputies. Cesare Rossi was then given the contract to do away with him. He organized the assassination, employing professional executioners, Filippelli and Dumini, to do the killing. A warrant against him was issued and Rossi was instructed by Mussolini to abscond. He took refuge in Naples with Piscitelli, one of the powerful men behind the scenes of the Fascist revolution, who later spirited him away to Switzerland, where it seems an attempt was made by Mussolini and Co. to drop him. Rossi was then accepted into the fold of anti-Fascist circles in exile. He disclosed to them the details of the Sinclair Oil deal and wrote an open letter to Mussolini on this and other embarrassing matters which was published in foreign newspapers. It was then decided to trap him. He was induced by Piscitelli to come to Italy for a secret meeting near the Swiss border, and here he was seized by the Italian police, tried for treason and sentenced to 30 years.

My impression was that he was telling the truth in all this – there being no reason why he shouldn't. I asked him why he had had Matteotti killed. He answered, with a shrug of the shoulders, to help Mussolini out, and keep in with him, as he was the boss. When I handed him over to the giggling, half-crazy prison screws in Poggio Reale, he remained imperturbable. I told them not to cut his hair off, or put him in their filthy prison pyjamas, as they do whenever they can, even when a prisoner is only being held on remand.

February 28

Already at the end of February, the winter is slipping away and the onset of the melancholy of spring is announced by the seller of broad beans, who passes under our windows, always at dusk, with the saddest of cries : '*A fava fresca!*' The warmth of the sun comes through and seeps into the cold walls, and the town wakes to new life. On sale now – and only in this season – is a pagan springtime cake, *pastiera Napolitana*, made with soft grain of all kinds, removed from their husks months before ripe, and cooked with orange blossom. There is a description of it by one of the Latin authors. The Vico Satriano, the narrow street overlooked by one side of our building, hums with activity as a great, vociferous spring-cleaning begins and unwanted objects of all kinds, chipped crockery, broken vessels, irreparable articles of furniture, follow the slops into the street. Everyone shouts, gesticulates and sings snatches of mournful love songs such as '*Ammore Busciardo*' (Love the traitor), and a boy has appeared at the street-corner beneath us selling for five lire a collection of twenty-five of the latest ballads, all of them dedicated to romantic frustration.

In the Villa Nazionale, the long sash of municipal gardens separating us from the Bay, the storytellers have been drawn out by the sun to take up their positions. Circles of small boys gather while their canvas backgrounds depicting the barbarities of the wars between the Christians and Infidels are set up. In front of these the *Cantastorie* stand and begin their chanted recitations of the deeds of Charlemagne and the Paladins. For ten centuries the invading armies have come and gone. Foreign kings have ruled in Naples, and enslaved its people. Revolutions have been drowned in blood. But nothing of this has made the slightest impression on the imagination or memory of the common man, nor called for the addition of anything to the storyteller's repertoire. This is all that the little audience that gathers as he begins to intone his narrative in the Villa Nazionale still wants to hear about. The Swabians, the Aragonese, the Bourbons and now the Germans have been instantly forgotten. Charlemagne and Roland live on – miraculously in spite of the cinema – which will nevertheless defeat them in the end.

Last Sunday the sun was so hot that the first of the water-sellers even came on the scene. These picturesque figures and the equipment they carry are hardly changed from representations of them in the frescoes of Pompeii. The water-seller sells *acqua ferrata*, which is powerfully flavoured with iron and drawn from a single hole in the ground somewhere in Santa Lucia. The water is contained as illustrated at Pompeii in rounded earthenware vessels (*mmommere*) shaped like a woman's breast – an excellent example of marketing ingenuity on the part of the ancients – and a cup of it costs three or four times the equivalent amount of wine. The water-seller also sells lemon squash, made on the spot with fresh lemons and a great display of dexterity with his enormous iron lemon-squeezers. A teaspoonful of bicarbonate of soda goes into the glass, causing a violent eruption of spume. Many of our soldiers – who regard all things foreign with suspicion – have found this an excellent remedy for hangovers.

'O spasso, they reject. This word, which embraces a huge variety of nuts and edible seeds of all kinds, many of them strange in appearance, enshrines a concept of leisurely festivity, the nearest one can get to it in translation being 'pastime'. There are stalls at weekends in the gardens now selling baked chick-peas, pine-nuts, peanuts, and above all pumpkin seeds which are roasted in ovens of pure copper, the seller attracting custom by tugging at frequent intervals on the cord of a steam whistle. Nothing of this collection of edible trifles which constitute 'O spasso, can be said to have

93

much taste, but chewing them promotes reflection. All these traditional attractions now face the competition of the black market, and its presence in the Villa is the one thing that brings this scene completely into our times. Side by side with the traditional stalls are the brazen displays of presumably looted American cigarettes: Camels (in Neapolitan 'the humped donkey'), Raleighs ('the bearded King'), Chesterfields (*'O cesso fetta* – the lavatory stinks).

Today on the Via San Pasquale I saw my first *pazzariello*, the 'joker' of antiquity, who is on the scene again because at last new businesses are being opened, and although explained away as a form of advertisement for the benefit of the illiterate, his real function is that of an exorcist. He is there to drive away evil spirits and cleanse the premises of the influence of the evil eye. Undoubtedly the *pazzariello* is there, too, in the Pompeii frescoes, but his costume these days dates from the Napoleonic wars and includes a cocked hat. He rushes into the shop or bar as soon as the doors are open for business lashing out in all directions with his stick and bounding about in time to the music of the two drummers and the piper who form his team. The office is hereditary; one is born a *pazzariello*, not made one.

March 3

A story has come to light of yet another almost incredible scheme dreamed up by A-Force – operating in enemy-occupied territory – which has ended in typical catastrophe. It seems likely that the germ of this macabre idea originated as a result of a circular sent to all units at about Christmas, worded in part as follows:

> From reports that have been received it is apparent that prostitution in occupied Italy, and Naples in particular, has reached a pitch greater than has ever been witnessed in Italy before. So much is this so that it has led to a suggestion that the encouragement of prostitution is part of a formu-

lated plan arranged by pro-Axis elements, primarily to spread venereal disease among Allied troops.

A-Force, mulling over this, would have known that the incidence of VD in German-occupied areas is very low indeed. This is partly because it is a criminal offence under Italian law, punishable by one year in prison, to communicate syphilis to a second person, and partly because the Germans have maintained the strictest of medical supervision over brothels. Thus, for one reason or another, the German-occupied North is virtually clear of streptococci and gonococci which to all intents and purposes were reintroduced into Italy with the arrival of the American troops. A-Force's plan was to arrange for the spread of these infections, which have reached epidemic levels in the South, across the lines into the uninfected North, and thus diminish the fighting efficiency of the German Army, while turning their backs on all such considerations as the suffering likely to be endured by the civilian population, and the many babies doomed to be born blind.

By the first week in January, a number of attractive young Neapolitan prostitutes had been rounded up, and of these twenty were selected, who, while showing no outward sign of infection, were believed by the medical men called in to co-operate with the A-Force scheme to be suffering from an exceptionally virulent and virtually ineradicable form of syphilis.

They were removed to a guarded villa in the Vomero, pampered in every way, given all the army white bread and spaghetti they could eat, taken on a day-trip to Capri – although of necessity denied any form of medical attention, apart from regular inspections to see that no unsightly chancres had developed. The news was then broken to them what was expected of them, and the trouble began. However many inducements were offered, they were naturally terrified at the idea of crossing the lines in the care of A-Force agents. Payment was to be made in the form of gold coins to be carried in the rectum, as well as original lira notes; but handsome as it was, the girls knew only too well how harsh was the economic climate of the North by comparison with Naples, and how hard and how risky it would be to make a living once the original bonuses were spent. One girl recruited from a staff of twelve resident prostitutes employed by the Albergo Vittoria, Sorrento, taken over as a rest hotel for American personnel, was accustomed to receive 1000 lire a night. In Rome she knew she would be lucky to earn 100 lire, and could not be convinced that her condition would long escape discovery by the German doctors.

But the main obstacle to the enterprise appears to have been an emotional one. All these girls had pimps from whom they could not bear to be parted. Some of the pimps were big enough in the scale of their professions, too, to be able to buy favours, and they were beginning to make trouble through AMGOT. Finally, like so many wild A-Force schemes, the thing was dropped, and the girls were then simply turned loose on the streets of Naples. The situation now is that as many hospital beds in the Naples area are occupied by sufferers from the pox as from wounds and all the other sicknesses put together.

March 5

Line-crossers become more and more active. Many of these people are driven by the determination – whatever the risk incurred – to be reunited with their families in German-occupied territory. No doubt just as many cross the lines coming in our direction. There is also an ever-increasing number of couriers, some working for the intelligence of either or both sides and others who simply carry letters backwards and forwards for financial reward. They work through agents who collect the letters from the ordinary Italian public. In the past all this was done with great secrecy, but now the line-crossers and their collectors are becoming careless. Only last week Signora Lola reported to me that if one wanted to send a letter to Rome a jeweller in the Via Roma would arrange for this to be done for a payment of 200 lire. From the security point of view this is a catastrophic situation, and one assumes that enemy agents in the liberated area have not the slightest difficulty in passing across the lines whatever information they may wish to send by using these people.

Within twenty-four hours of receiving Lola's information and before any action could be taken, both Lattarullo and Losurdo supplied the name of a letter-carrier – Giovanni Patierno – who was soon tracked down. As it turned out, Patierno was being used as a guide by A-Force agents, and had also been involved in the ill-conceived scheme to take the twenty prostitutes infected with syphilis across the line and deliver them to Rome. With A-Force's unwonted collaboration Patierno was picked up this morning in the Café Savoia, Piazza Dante – a rendezvous, it appears, of such dubious characters. The occasion was a picturesque one. We borrowed a half-dozen Pubblica Sicurezza agents, all of them dressed like detectives in an old René Clair film, in boaters, bow-ties, and in two cases even spats. These surrounded the café, charged in with drawn pistols, and arrested everyone in sight. Besides Patierno, several other line-crossers were pulled in, but as they all worked for A-Force, they were let go. Patierno, charged with his misdeeds, instantly caved in, took us back to his flat and showed us a stove full of charred remnants of the letters he had been paid up to a thousand lire to deliver. He was a horrible, weasel-faced little man. It is remarkable how really despicable villainy like this shows so often in the face. A few letters collected that day hadn't been destroyed. They were from the social, commercial and religious elite of Naples, and it has been decided that nothing will be done about them, although under the proclamation huge penalties are prescribed for illegalities of this kind.

The collecting agents were in a different case, and we were flabbergasted to discover that one of these was the famous midget gynæcologist Professore Dottore Salerno – already

known to Parkinson – who is said to employ a tiny step-ladder
to work at his gynæcologist couch. Salerno is supposed to
come from one of the celebrated families of cabinet-makers
of Sorrento, whose eldest sons traditionally became surgeons,
having been encouraged by the traditions of the family trade
to develop extreme manual dexterity at an early age. In his
case this traditional skill has been fostered by Salerno's ability
to work with both hands where necessary in the female pelvic
cavity. We called forthwith on the Professore, shook the tiny
paw he extended, and I looked on and listened while he and
Parkinson exchanged endless courtesies before the bad news
was broken. The Professore was told that we should be obliged
to search his elegant curio-packed house, and not a muscle
moved in the wizened little monkey face. While the search went
on the Professore skipped along at our side, entertaining us
with a stream of urbane and witty conversation. Nothing was
found. Salerno was far too wily a bird to be caught like this.
Nor in the absence of concrete and damning evidence could
a man of the Professore's social status and power be successfully prosecuted. We apologized, shook hands once more, and
said goodbye, and the Professore invited us to dinner. A bishop
from Sicily would be there. One wondered why on earth a man
of Salerno's standing had ever got himself mixed up in a thing
like this.

From the Professore's house we went straight to Rufo, the
jeweller's shop in the Via Roma, and here we were luckier,
finding several letters awaiting collection by Patierno. As for
the deplorable Patierno himself, there was nothing really we
could do about him, as the fraud he'd practised on his fellow
citizens was no business of ours. He was therefore released,
and left to the fury of his victims, who would certainly not
be long in finding out what had happened.

March 13

The war on the black market is being conducted with spurts

of ferocity, but the victims who fall are always and only those who have no one to speak out for them, and cannot bribe their way out of their predicament. Whole shiploads of army stores are spirited away, and items from these can be bought by every Italian civilian who has the money to pay. I am convinced it would be impossible to stop and search a single Neapolitan in the street without finding that he was wearing an overcoat or jacket made from army blankets, or army underclothing, army socks, or at the least had American cigarettes in his pocket.

Attended yesterday at the Castello Capuano for the trial of the Rufo brothers charged with acting as agents for the smuggling of letters into enemy-held territory. This proved to be a farce. The prosecutor had not familiarized himself with the case, did not know which of the persons had been brought to trial and had lost the translations of the letters. Result : the Rufos got off with two months apiece. Another Commendatore of the Crown of Italy got a year for possession of a large quantity of stolen Allied supplies, but was released on bail. At the appeal he will be defended by Lelio Porzio, who now charges 20,000 lire, and is certain to get the man off.

The reverse of the coin is the case of the dock-workers rounded up by the MPs and found in possession of rations. They had broken open a case and helped themselves to about half a dozen tins apiece. One of them was put in the dock to be got rid of while legal arguments were going on over the Rufos. He was chained up in the usual way, weeping desperately, clearly knowing what was coming. It took the judge minutes to find him guilty and sentence him to ten years. 'What's going to happen to my poor family?' he shrieked. He was led away sobbing loudly. A sickening experience.

March 14

Today another horrible example of what can happen to the poor when the army decides on a counter-offensive on the black market. A boy of about ten was brought into the 92nd General Hospital by his distracted mother. He'd had three fingers chopped off. These she handed over, wrapped up in newspaper, with the request that they be sewn on again. Somebody had told her that only the British were capable of this kind of surgery. The story was that this little boy was one of a juvenile gang that specialized in jumping into the backs of army lorries when held up in traffic and snatching up anything pilferable. We heard that they had been dealt with by having a man with a bayonet hidden under a taurpaulin in the back of every supply-lorry. As soon as a boy grabbed the tailboard to haul himself in, the waiting soldier chopped down at his hands. God knows how many children have lost their fingers in this way.

March 15

A bad raid last night with heavy civilian casualties, as usual, in the densely populated port areas. I was sent this morning to investigate the reports of panic, and frantic crowds running through the streets crying, 'Give us peace,' and 'Out with all the soldiers.' In Santa Lucia, home territory of the Neapolitan ballad, I saw a heart-rending scene. A number of tiny children had been dug out of the ruins of a bombed building and lay side by side in the street. Where presentable, their faces were uncovered, and in some cases brand-new dolls had been thrust into their arms to accompany them to the other world. Professional mourners, hired by the locality to reinforce the grief of the stricken families, were running up and down the street, tearing at their clothing and screaming horribly. One man climbed into the rubble and was calling into a hole where he believed his little boy was trapped under hundreds of tons of masonry, begging him not to die before he could be dug out. 'Hang on, son. Only a few minutes longer now. We'll have you out of there in a minute. Please don't die.' The Germans murder only the poor in these indiscriminate raids, just as we did.

There has been an issue to the troops of leaflets printed in Italian to be handed to any tout approaching a soldier to offer the services of a prostitute. It begins : 'I am not interested in your syphilitic sister.' Whoever dreamed this one up clearly had no idea of some of the implications or the possible consequences. Remarks about sisters are strictly taboo to Southern Italians, and the final insult *tu sora* (thy sister) is calculated instantly to produce a duel or vendetta. Many soldiers have already handed over these dangerous notices to people who accosted them for reasons other than prostitution, and there are bound to be casualties.

March 19

Today Vesuvius erupted. It was the most majestic and terrible sight I have ever seen, or ever expect to see. The smoke from the crater slowly built up into a great bulging shape having all the appearance of solidity. It swelled and expanded so slowly that there was no sign of movement in the cloud which, by evening, must have risen thirty or forty thousand feet into the sky, and measured many miles across.

The shape of the eruption that obliterated Pompeii reminded Pliny of a pine tree, and he probably stood here at Posillipo across the bay, where I was standing now and where Nelson and Emma Hamilton stood to view the eruption of their day, and the shape was indeed like that of a many-branching tree. What took one by surprise about Pliny's pine was that it was absolutely motionless, not quite painted – because it was three-dimensional – but moulded on the sky; an utterly still, and utterly menacing shape. This pine, too, trailed uncharacteristically a little tropical liana of heavy ash, which fell earthwards here and there from its branches in imperceptible motion.

At night the lava streams began to trickle down the mountain's slopes. By day the spectacle was calm but now the eruption showed a terrible vivacity. Fiery symbols were scrawled across the water of the bay, and periodically the crater discharged mines of serpents into a sky which was the deepest of blood reds and pulsating everywhere with lightning reflections.

March 20

Today the sky was fogged over and ash was falling, and everything – the buildings, streets and fields – was covered to a depth of a half-inch in a smooth grey pall. At Sorrento, and on Capri and Ischia the ash lay already in places several inches deep. There was fear for the safety of military installations in areas such as Portici and Torre del Greco which always suffer the worst effects of an eruption of Vesuvius, and I was instructed to find out what the prospects were – if these could in any way be gauged – of a worsening in the situation.

I drove out in a slow, grey, snowfall to visit Professor Saraceno, a leading seismologist who showed himself pleasantly excited at the prospect of the vindication of certain of his theories. He said that the destruction of Pompeii probably followed the undercutting by the eruption of those days of part of the crater wall. This eventually fell into the crater, sealing off for a time the eruptive forces until such time as pressure built up to produce an explosion which discharged millions of tons of pulverized rock into the air. From an inspection he had made of the crater some months previously, he believed a disaster of the same kind could be repeated, and I got the impression that he would not be wholly dismayed if it were. I thanked him sincerely, and repaid his advice with a tin of corned beef, which he accepted with gratitude.

March 22

An increase in the violence of the eruption, and also of the population's fears. Following the news that San Sebastiano was about to be carried away by the lava stream, and Cercola was threatened, I was sent to get an on-the-spot report.

Sticky going all the way through the ash, with several skids. At San Giorgio a road-block had been put up and all vehicles not concerned with the emergency were being turned back. There were reports in this area of showers of the small volcanic stones technically known as *lapilli*, and here and there larger rocks had fallen, causing so far one death. At this point I was right under the great grey cloud, full of swellings and protuberances, like some colossal pulsating brain.

Reaching San Sebastiano, it seemed incredible that all its people could have consented to go on living in such a position. The town was built at the very tip of a tongue of land until now spared by the volcano, but completely outflanked by the tremendous lava fields left by the eruption of 1872, and in effect lying in a valley between them. There were nine major eruptions in the last century alone, lava being on several occasions discharged in this direction, while lava streams have frequently burst forth from lateral openings at lower levels on the slopes. Here, stranded as it was in the no-man's-land of the volcano, any outsider would have predicted the town's eventual destruction as a matter of mathematical certainty, yet apparently no citizen of San Sebastiano would admit even to the possibility of this. Civic permanency is a matter of religious faith. Buildings are solidly constructed to withstand the centuries. Slow-growing trees are planted. Main-street businesses advertise with pride the age of their establishment. The population creeps up numerically and the young people stay on. All windows face westwards in hope across green valleys towards Naples, and the houses turn their backs on the grey eternal cone of the volcano. San Sebastiano fights back with colour against the ashen desert of old lava that almost encircles it. Even in wartime I found it a well-painted place, with geraniums in window-boxes everywhere, and an additional liveliness provided by the political parties with their posters and their flags.

At the time of my arrival the lava was pushing its way very quietly down the main street, and about fifty yards from the edge of this great, slowly-shifting slagheap, a crowd of several hundred people, mostly in black, knelt in prayer. Holy banners and church images were held aloft, and acolytes swung censers and sprinkled holy water in the direction of the cinders. Occasionally a grief-crazed citizen would grab one of the banners and dash towards the wall of lava, shaking it angrily as if to warn off the malignant spirits of the eruption. The spectacle of the eruption was totally unexpected. I had been prepared for rivers of fire, but there was no fire and no burning anywhere – only the slow, deliberate suffocation of the town under millions of tons of clinkers. The lava was moving at a rate of only a few yards an hour, and it had covered half the town to a depth of perhaps thirty feet. A complete, undamaged cupola of a church, severed from the submerged building, jogged slowly towards us on its bed of cinders. The whole process was strangely quiet. The black slagheap shook, trembled and jerked a little and cinders rattled down its slope. A house, cautiously encircled and then overwhelmed, disappeared from sight intact, and a faint, distant grinding sound followed as the lava began its digestion. As I watched, a tall building housing what was clearly the town's smart café took the pressure of the lava's movement. For perhaps fifteen or twenty minutes it resisted, then the juddering, trembling spasm of the lava seemed to pass into its fabric, and it, too, began to tremble, before its walls bulged and it went down.

Dominant in every way, for sheer size, and the number of persons supporting the platform of the images confronting the eruption, was that of San Sebastiano himself, but wandering away into a side street, I noticed the presence of another image, also with numerous attendants, which was covered with a white sheet. One of the Carabinieri patrolling on the look-out for looters told me that this was an image of San Gennaro, smuggled in from Naples on an outside chance that it might be of some use if all else failed. It had been covered with a sheet to avoid offence to the confraternity of San Sebastiano and the Saint himself who might have been expected to resent this intrusion into his territory. As the last resort only, San Gennaro would be brought into the open and implored to perform a miracle. The Carabiniere did not think this would be necessary, because it was clear to him that the lava stream was slowing down.

We strolled back together into the main street, and in fact there had been no advance that I could detect within the last hour. The café had gone, but the cinema next door was still there, protected now by a dozen young men who had formed a line and had advanced, brandishing crosses, to within a few yards of the lava. Not a single clinker tumbled down the black slope as we watched. Flakes of ash, softer than snow, were still drifting down, but the day seemed to have lightened, and for a moment the sunlit cone of the volcano came into sight ahead, as if through a tear in a curtain. Childish voices somewhere in the rear had begun to sing a *Te Deum*. It seemed likely that half the town would be saved.

March 24

It was clear today that the eruption had lost its force, and the news was that roughly half San Sebastiano had in fact been spared.

I visited Lattarullo who introduced me to a friend, Carlo Del Giudice, another non-practising lawyer who made an incredibly precarious living by writing newspaper articles on folk-lore and astronomy. He got an article published once or twice a month and, taking devaluation into account, received about the equivalent of one pound for each contribution. Like

Lattarullo, he lived on cups of coffee substitute, pumpkin seeds and an occasional pizza, and smoked cigarettes made up by real craftsmen from ends collected in the street. These some people even prefer to straightforward Camels, Chesterfields and Lucky Strikes, as having more flavour. Unlike Lattarullo, starvation had not made him stringy and emaciated, but produced a kind of puffy inflation. He looked hollow.

Del Giudice was an expert on the subject of San Gennaro, and therefore Vesuvius, as the two were linked together, and had privately published a little book dealing with the scientific and natural explanations of miracles. Neither he nor any of his friends, all of them connoisseurs of eruptions, had been allowed to get anywhere near Vesuvius, so he was delighted to be able to talk to someone who had viewed the eruption at close quarters and enquired into every detail of my experiences at San Sebastiano. Above all, he was most interested to hear of an image of San Gennaro being kept round a corner out of sight, ready to go into action in a final emergency.

According to the opinion of most Neapolitans, Del Giudice said, it wouldn't have made the slightest difference if it had. San Gennaro had confined his miracle-working to Naples for fourteen centuries since his martyrdom at Pozzuoli and it was believed of him that he wouldn't lift a finger to save the rest of the world from destruction. San Gennaro's job had been to keep the fires of Vesuvius at bay, but only on behalf of Naples. During this period Resina and Torre Del Greco, only five and seven miles respectively down the coast, had been overwhelmed by lava and rebuilt seven times.

He personally was a sceptic and a rationalist, Del Giudice said, and Lattarullo nodded approval; he was too. However, three people out of four – and he included the educated classes – were openly or secretly of the belief that Naples could only be protected from Vesuvius with San Gennaro on its side. He cited the one period in history when Naples had tried to change saints, and what the consequences had been. In 1799 Napoleon's troops took Naples, and the Saint was involved in the resistance to the occupation. It was made clear through the priests of his cult that the miraculous liquefaction of his congealed blood kept in an ampulla in the Cathedral would not take place on the first Saturday in May, as it had always done. As the prosperity of Naples was always believed to depend on this recurrent miracle, riots began, and French soldiers were assassinated. At eight in the evening of the day when the miracle was due to take place, and the crowds were howling and rampaging in the streets, a French staff-officer went to the officiating priest and gave him ten minutes to produce the miracle, or be shot. The blood promptly liquefied but San Gennaro, charged by the Neapolitans with collaboration, was dismissed and his image thrown into the sea. He was replaced by San Antonio Abate, chosen as the heaven-appointed guardian against fire, but it turned out that the only fires he could prevent or suppress – and according to Del Giudice he was immensely successful in this way during his tenure of office – were those of man-made origin. From historical evidence, he said, private houses practically ceased to burn down with San Antonio in control, but in dealing with the first eruption of the volcano he proved to be out of his depth, and with the lava rolling towards the city fishermen were sent to drag the sea-bed and recover the image of San Gennaro. There was a moment of crisis while the fisherman searched unsuccessfully for the image, which by then had been in the water for several years, but in the nick of time a statue of the saint which had been erected on the Maddaloni Bridge and had somehow been forgotten came to the rescue, raising and spreading its marble arms to halt the passage of the lava. With this miraculous happening, reported to have been witnessed by thousands, the day of San Antonio was at an end, and San Gennaro was back again.

People, Del Giudice said, will believe anything.

March 25

Fear is expressed that the blood of San Gennaro may refuse to liquefy this year, and that such a failure might be exploited by secret anti-Allied factions and troublemakers to set off large-scale rioting of the kind that has frequently happened in Neapolitan history when the miracle has failed. Everywhere there is a craving for miracles and cures. The war has pushed the Neapolitans back into the Middle Ages. Churches are suddenly full of images that talk, bleed, sweat, nod their heads and exude health-giving liquors to be mopped up by handkerchiefs, or even collected in bottles, and anxious, ecstatic crowds gather waiting for these marvels to happen. Every day the newspapers report new miracles. In the church of Santo Agnello, a speaking crucifix carries on a regular conversation with the image of Santa Maria d'Intercessione – a fact confirmed by reporters on the spot. The image of Santa Maria del Carmine, first recorded as having bowed its head to avoid a cannot-shot during the siege of Naples by Alfonso of Aragon, now does this as a matter of daily routine. This church used to be visited annually by the King and his court to watch the royal barber shave the hair that had miraculously grown on an ivory Christ during the preceding twelve months. The custom is likely to be renewed. And even if San Gennaro's blood doesn't liquefy they have a phial of the blood of St John in San Giovanni a Carbonara, which – say the papers – bubbles away every time the gospel is read to it.

The woman who cooks for us mentioned today that she would be taking time off to visit the chapel of Sant' Aspreno. She suffers from neuralgia and expects to obtain relief by pushing her head through a hole in the wall of the chapel. The Saint is patron of sufferers from headaches, and there are daily queues at the chapel waiting to be able to submit themselves to this treatment. Naples has reached a state of nervous exhaustion when mass hallucination has become a commonplace, and belief of any kind can be more real than reality.

March 26

The streets of Naples are full of people hawking personal possessions of all kinds : pieces of jewellery, old books, pictures, clothing, etc. Many of them are members of the middle class, and the approach is made in a shamefaced and surreptitious way. One and all, they are in a state of desperate need.

Today at the top of the Via Roma near the Piazza Dante I was stopped by a pleasant-faced old lady, who had nothing for sale but who implored me to go with her to her house in a side-street nearby. She had something to show me, and was so insistent that I followed her to the typical *basso* in a side-street, where she lived. The single, windowless room was lit by a minute electric bulb over the usual shrine, and I saw a thin girl standing in a corner. The reason for the appeal now became clear. This, said the woman, was her child, aged thirteen, and she wished to prostitute her. Many soldiers, it seems, will pay for sexual activity less than full intercourse, and she had a revolting scale of fees for these services. For example, the girl would strip and display her pubescent organs for twenty lire.

I told the woman that I would report her to the police, and she pretended to weep, but it was an empty threat, and she knew it. Nothing can be done. There are no police to deal with the thousands of squalid little crimes like this committed every day in the city.

On my way back I was stopped and drawn into a corner by a priest, white-lipped and smiling. He opened a bag full of umbrella handles, candlesticks and small ornaments of all kinds carved out of the bones of the saints, i.e. from bones filched from one of the catacombs. He, too, had to live.

Apart from negative definitions by GHQ (FS personnel will

in no circumstances be used as interpreters), nobody seems quite to know what we are and what we do. As a result any job that no other branch of the forces wants to tackle is automatically thrown in our direction. It is now announced that we will investigate and report on all applications by Italian females in the Naples area to marry British soldiers. This will entail collecting information from the competitive and mutually hostile Pubblica Sicurezza Police, and the Carabinieri, questioning the applicant herself, and appraising the circumstances and the environment in which she lives.

This is a chore nobody in the section seems anxious to take on, so it falls to my lot.

March 29

Miracles galore in the past few days. At the weekend crowds flocked out to the Campi Flegrei to watch the performance of a 12-year-old local Bernadette to whom the Virgin has appeared several times with comforting messages for the population. A band was in attendance, and in the absence of any more suitable form of transport, the Sindaco of Marano arrived in a motor-hearse.

At Pomigliano we have a flying monk* who also demonstrates the stigmata. The monk claims that on an occasion last year when an aerial dog-fight was in progress, he soared up to the sky to catch in his arms the pilot of a stricken Italian plane, and bring him safely to earth. Most of the Neapolitans I know – some of them educated men – are convinced of the truth of this story.

April 1

An excursion with Frazer, the Signora Lola and friend in the naval launch carrying supplies to Capri. Frazer as stylish-looking and emaciated as ever in his well-cut battle blouse

* This man became the celebrated Padre Pio.

and Desert Rat polka-dotted scarf; Lola beautifully bloated through the return of *pasta* to the menus of Naples. Her friend, Susanna, was a frisky red-head of about twenty-five, the possessor of a mime so expressive that within minutes, and hardly a word passing between them, she was able to give Frazer a brief outline of her life history. Both ladies were absurdly dressed for the occasion in fox furs, with small straw hats decorated with glass fruit on top of their piled-up tresses.

It was one of those golden mornings of Naples. Within minutes of chugging out of the harbour, the town behind us was afloat in layers of mist, and all its strong colours, its reds and its corals, faded to a pacific grey. After that a headland with pines showing like a pencil drawing, the tops of towers, the Castel Sant' Elmo in suspension over the town, then utter dazzlement. Frazer produced a loaf and cut it up to cries of girlish delight. This party was as much about bread as it was about Capri – an excuse for the ladies to eat limitless white bread under picnic conditions. They munched the bread and laughed uproariously, and threw mangled crusts to the escorting seagulls. An unlicensed fishing-boat veered nervously away trailing a little mandolin music, and ahead Capri penetrated a quilt of mist like the tip of a volcano.

Capri, like hashish, is supposed to bring out the demon, whatever its nature, lurking at the bottom of the human personality, and people go ashore at the Marina Grande hypnotized in advance by its reputation. Frazer disposed of his supplies and we went up to the village and sat in a café in the Piazza Municipio. This was a different world from Naples; escapist, full of make-believe, and almost hysterically concerned to show its lack of interest in the war. Civilians find it difficult to get passes for the island, but all the old Capri-hands were there; the men dressed to go shooting and the women in sandals and streaming veils like Isadora Duncan just about to go off on the last fatal trip in the Bugatti.

We ordered the inevitable marsala – the alternative being a local gin that smelt of turps – and the girls took the bread they had saved from their beaded handbags, and began to chew. The waiter counted in German, and went off, saying *Danke* for the tip, and we settled into our roles in the pageant of Capri. An American major at the next table sat with his arms round the waists of a couple of courtesans singing a blustering version of '*Torna a Sorrento*', and when the municipal loudspeakers began to blast out a tarantella one of them was persuaded to hop about in what was supposed to be a dance on the table-top. A hanger-on I knew vaguely from Naples attached himself to point out Madame Four-Dollars, a foreign expatriate so-called from her fixed price paid to fisherman for sexual services, and to invite us to visit the Villa Tiberius, whose ancient scandals were part of the island's stock-in-trade. The haunted face of Curzio Malaparte whom I believed to be in the internment camp of Padula but from which he had clearly been released, appeared briefly, and among his courtiers I observed a British officer who, under the spell of his environment, grimaced and gesticulated in all directions.

So far the trip had been a huge success. This was Life as far as both girls were concerned, and Frazer, from the cautious nonconformist background of Peebles, had to admit that he'd never imagined that such a place as Capri could exist. Then suddenly there were agitated whisperings, confusion broke out at our table, and both girls got up, flustered away into the café and disappeared. Frazer, who went after them, came back perplexed. They had both left the café by the back entrance, and disappeared. While we were discussing the strange behaviour we noticed a small grey-haired Italian sitting at a table across the street, who was staring malevolently at us, and I felt that his presence must have had something to do with the girls' panic-stricken departure.

We wandered about the village which is too small to be a hiding-place, and in the end we found the fugitives and listened with what polite pretence of belief we could to the story concocted by Lola to explain what had happened. The venomous-looking little Italian had been an old family friend who had conceived a passion for her, and continued to pursue her hopelessly, to follow her, to make her life miserable by turning up like this out of the blue, despite the fact that she had told him a hundred times she never wanted to see him again. The relationship, she assured Frazer, tears welling in her enormous innocent eyes, had never been anything other than platonic. It was my task to translate all these protestations followed by the cross-fire of accusation and denial.

Later, when the girls had been shipped back to Naples and delivered to their homes, Frazer wanted to know how much of Lola's story I believed, and it seemed to me a disservice not to tell him what I knew. The angry little man was a director of the Banco di Napoli, I told him, and had been a high official of the Fascist government, although not quite high enough for him to qualify for internment. 'Do you think he's still her lover?' he wanted to know.

'How does she live? How does she eat? Where did the fox furs come from? You don't keep her. Why live in a fool's paradise?'

'I've never met a beautiful woman like Lola before,' Frazer said. 'I thought she loved me.'

'She does,' I said. 'But one day, sooner or later, you'll be posted away, and she'll have to go on living here. What do you expect her to do, starve? Work in a factory? Love's all very well but she has to live.'

'I suppose she does, but I don't think I ought to see her again.'

'That's for you to decide,' I told him.

April 3

Frazer came round to HQ today, obviously distraught, and we went to the Vittoria for a drink. He seemed to have come to terms with the knowledge that he had been sharing Lola's sexual favours with the ex-Federale, and would continue to share them while the relationship persisted, but was very worried about an attack made upon her by the other man, which in his opinion amounted to attempted murder.

His story was that, subsequent to our trip to Capri, Lola refused to see him for three days, and when in the end she finally appeared, her neck was terribly bruised.

I reassured him. This was what is known locally as a *strozzamento di amanti* – a lovers' semi-throttling. It was a form – a convention almost – in such relationships, and was tolerated and even appreciated as a proof of passion by Neapolitan girls, whereas a *schiaffeggiamento*, or beating up, was not. Had the bank director beaten her up, the chances were that she might have left him there and then, which meant that she would have had to turn to him, Frazer, for her support. 'Ask yourself,' I said. 'Do you think you could take on the exclusive rights on a basis of £10 a week?'

'No,' he said. 'I don't. I think I'll have to give her up.'

April 5

Twenty-eight investigations of prospective brides for Servicemen completed to date, of which twenty-two proved to be prostitutes. Of these, seven were officially described as such in the dossiers of the Pubblica Sicurezza or the Carabinieri. The rest were obviously living on immoral earnings because – in surroundings of total poverty and hunger – they and their houses were clean and well-kept, their children, if they had any, were shod, and there was food in the larder.

Always the same question. 'Where does the money come from?' To this there is an almost standard reply. 'My uncle sends me some.' I ask for the uncle's address, explaining that I am bound to check up, and this produces a sad smile, and a shrug of the shoulders. The game is up. There is no such uncle.

'Can you do anything for me?' the girl usually wants to know. 'I didn't ask to live like this. Give me the chance to get away from it and I'll be as good a wife as anybody else.'

The Bureau of Psychological Warfare has just stated in its bulletin that there are 42,000 women in Naples engaged either on a regular or occasional basis in prostitution. This out of a nubile female population of perhaps 150,000. It seems incredible. Three out of four of these girls I have interviewed will probably cease to be prostitutes as soon as they can hope to keep alive by any other means. One would like to be able to do something for these applicants to marry our soldiers. Of the twenty-two failed candidates most seemed kindly, cheerful, and hard-working at their household tasks, and their standard of good looks was very high. Nine out of ten Italian girls have lost their menfolk, who have either disappeared in battles, into prisoner-of-war camps, or been cut off in the North. The whole population is out of work. Nobody produces anything. How are they to live? Some Neapolitans have not tasted meat for two years. The marvel is that these girls can actually find a male once in a way – apart from soldiers – able to pay the very small sums they are ready to accept for their services.

April 7

To Nola to interview five British privates waiting to be reposted to their units at the GRTD there, who escaped from a German prison camp near Terni and came in safely a few days ago.

All these had picked up enough basic Italian to be able to persuade the Italians working in the camp to bring in odds and ends of civilian clothing, which they stashed away until each man could dress himself up as an Italian civilian. The Italians did this out of the goodness of their hearts. Not only did they give away garments which they would probably have been glad to keep for themselves, but they exposed themselves to a terrific risk in doing what they did. Workers were put through some sort of perfunctory search both when arriving at the camp and leaving, and parcels were opened, so the spare items of clothing had to be worn. A man would come in wearing two pairs of trousers or two shirts, or he would stick a pair of canvas-soled shoes into his jacket pocket, leave his boots behind with the British prisoner, and wear these to go out. When all was ready the escapees quietly mixed in with the Italian workers and walked out through the gates. One of them described a tense moment when a guard didn't seem to recognize his face, and stopped him, but was quite happy to let him go on being assured in broken Italian, '*Noi lavorare per voi.*'

Thereafter the five calmly set out on their 150-mile walk back to our lines. The journey was undertaken in the most leisurely and relaxed fashion and there was nothing furtive about it. When they saw Germans ahead they kept up their stolid march, ready to wave, smile and shout encouragements in their broken Italian. Before their capture they'd listened to a standard S-Force lecture on how to handle a situation like this, and had noted the recommendation never to go to the big house in any village for help or food, but to rely on the poor, 'because they have nothing to lose'. In fact they had their lives to lose – because the Germans gave short shrift to shelterers of escaped prisoners – but none of the Italians who helped our five friends to get back gave any thought to that. Progress was much slowed down because one of the party had a poisoned foot, and could only make a small number of miles a day, so the journey took over two weeks. When the men were hungry they would decide on a small house they liked the look of in a village street, knock on the door, explain who they were, and ask for food. In no case was this ever denied them. After they had eaten they were often offered beds for the night, and for this purpose were shared out among the neighbours. Sometimes they were urged to stay as long as they liked – in one case to settle down and become members of the local community. Money was pressed on them. The old people in Italian villages treated them as sons, and the young ones as brothers.

It turned out that there were several more soldiers in the depot at Nola who had had experiences of this kind, and I spent some hours talking to them. To date I have not heard of a single instance of escaping British soldiers being betrayed to the Germans. This adds to the general impression of the civilization and impressive humanity of our Italian ex-enemies. For this reason, since humanity is above partisanship, the Italians are no doubt equally kind to Germans who come to them for help in similar circumstances, and I find it deplorable that we should show anger and vindictiveness when cases of Italians showing even ordinary compassion to their one-time allies come to our notice.

Recently a case was reported in the bulletin of the Psychological Warfare Bureau of Italian women near Avezzano who came out of their houses to offer wine to German prisoners under escort, resting while on the march. The writer took this as evidence of the existence in those parts of dangerous pro-German sentiments and was properly wrathful over the incident.

April 14

Five more marriage vettings this week, one of them extraordinary.

To Santa Maria della Colombina to investigate a Contessa della Peruta who wished to marry a British officer. Both Pubblica Sicurezza and Carabinieri agreed (for once) on favourable reports. There were no gross scandals whispered by the neighbours, so I went to see the Contessa who lived in a huge house – practically a castle – dominating the village. I was shown by a smart little maid into a room furnished with tapestry and antiques, which came as a pleasant change after the majority of Italian country houses, which – even in the case of the upper classes – are usually bare and austere.

After rather a long wait the Contessa appeared, with apologies and smiles. Even by Italian standards she was beautiful, with fine features and regal manners, and dressed with quiet elegance. We had a short talk in which she showed liveliness and charm. For the first time I found myself envying the man involved, and I went back to HQ to turn in an almost lyrical report.

Four days later – by the greatest of chances – I found myself in Santa Maria again, engaged in some routine enquiry, and it occurred to me that having a contact there, who might be able to help, I should call on the Contessa again. After hammering on the door for some minutes I was admitted by a half-starved-looking crone into the vast room, now hardly recognizable as it was completely empty. A long wait while the Contessa was found. She was still as beautiful as ever but dressed in a coarse jumper and skirt. She burst into tears and the truth came out. One neighbour had lent the empty house. Three more had provided the furniture for the single room. Others had chipped in with articles of clothing. Although a member of an ancient aristocratic family, she possessed no more than any other impoverished village girl in her own right.

I consoled her with assurances that the report had already been completed, and the marriage would almost certainly go through. One of the good neighbours rushed in with the inevitable marsala. Toasts were drunk to the bride and lucky bridegroom-to-be, and I went on my way.

April 15

Today for the first time a marriage candidate gave me an absolutely straight answer to the question, 'Where does the money come from?'

She was a neat, pleasant, smiling girl, and what instantly gave her away was the bar of soap in the kitchen of her tiny flat off the Via Chiaia. This was worth a small fortune at present black-market prices, and most girls still clean themselves by rubbing their skins with pumice and ashes. A bottle on the shelf contained about a half-pint of olive oil, the presence of this almost priceless commodity strengthening my suspicions to the point of certainty.

Calmly and smilingly she announced that an Italian major and an American corporal contributed to her support. She added that the corporal's army pay was ten times that of the major, who seemed to be tolerated in a good-natured way as an old client she was not prepared to dismiss because he'd fallen on hard times, rather than as a source of income.

I took the trouble to verify her facts and found that an Italian major is currently paid 3063 lire a month. This with the lira fixed at 400 to the pound comes to £7 10s. While I was about it I looked into some other wages. The Questore of Naples, holding a rank equal to that of major-general, is at the top of the list of civil servants and is paid 5496 lire. At the bottom, a postman gets 450 lire. Thus a man with a wife and an average five children to provide for, as well as the two or three old folk included in the normal Italian family, has to perform the miracle of keeping them all alive on just over one pound a month.

The Italians of the South live, just as Africans do, on bread dipped in olive oil. These days bread bought on the black market, and made with bad-quality dirty flour, fetches 160 lire a kilogram. Four shillings in London buys as many loaves as 600 lire on the black market in Naples. Olive oil costs 450 lire a litre, eggs 30 lire each, and salt cannot be bought at any price.

Considering these figures, it seems extraordinary that the Neapolitans have the strength to walk, let alone work, and that one does not actually see them dying of starvation in the street.

April 18

The black market flourishes as never before. According to the Psychological Warfare Bureau's bulletin 65 per cent of the *per capita* income of Neapolitans derives from transactions in stolen Allied supplies, and one-third of all supplies and equipment imported continued to disappear into the black market. Every single item of Allied equipment, short of guns and munitions – which are said to be sold under the counter – is openly displayed for sale in the Forcella market. It was noted that at the opening of the San Carlo opera *every* middle- and upperclass woman arrived dressed in a coat made from a stolen army blanket. How easy it would be to trace all these articles back to the original thieves. When I suggested ways and means in which this could be done I was told by the FSO that the black market is none of our business.

Indeed, it is becoming generally known that it operates under the protection of high-placed Allied Military Government officials. One soon finds that however many underlings are arrested – and sent away these days for long terms of imprisonment – those who employ them are beyond the reach of the law. At the head of AMG is Colonel Charles Poletti, and working with him is Vito Genovese, once head of the American Mafia, now become his adviser. Genovese was born in a village near Naples, and has remained in close contact with its underworld, and it is clear that many of the Mafia-Camorra sindacos who have been appointed in the surrounding towns are his nominees. These facts, once State secrets, are now known to the Neapolitan man in the street. Yet nothing is done. However many damaging reports are put in about the activities of high-ranking AMG officials, they stay where they are.

The latest story going the rounds about 'a certain high-ranking AMG official' describes the trick played on him by the wife of a well-known industrialist. It appeared that this man had been sentenced to a year for dealing in stolen Allied goods. His wife went to the 'Beacon', the best of the Neapolitan brothels, and asked for the loan of their most intelligent girl. She dressed her in her smartest clothing, lent her her jewels, and paid 4000 lire for the girl to impersonate her, the wife, and to visit the said official to plead for the husband's freedom. The visit was a success and two days later the gates of Poggio Reale prison swung open for the industrialist.

The average Neapolitan's comment when hearing this typically Neapolitan story is, 'What a pity she didn't send a girl with the syphilis.'

April 24

Ran into Frazer again yesterday and found him handsome and haggard as ever, and in the same bemused condition over his continuing romance with the Signora Lola – who has long ceased to consult me in matters arising out of her emotional life. She had by now taught him to speak a little Italian of the kind lisped enchantingly by Neapolitan children just out of babyhood, in which all verbs are used in the infinitive and everybody, regardless of age and status, is addressed as *tu*. He had made a great business of breaking off the affair after our visit to Capri, and the discovery of the existence of another lover. Now after terrible scenes, recriminations, everlasting farewells, and a pretence of suicide on Lola's part, they were together again, but in conditions which sounded for Frazer more arduous than before. Lola had agreed to cut the Neapolitan banker out of her life for ever, and to give up the *iniezioni ricostituenti*, and Frazer had dictated the letter by which his rival was dismissed. In return Frazer had agreed to placing the relationship on a formal basis. She had become officially his *fidanzata*, and he had been compelled to buy her a ring that had cost him more than he could afford, and was set with a lack-lustre diamond he was sure was false. It was evident that he was deep in the Neapolitan quicksands, for she had next insisted that he should quite illegally requisition an empty flat in the fashionable Rione Amedeo, and he had weakly agreed. Operations of this kind have to be carried off with a certain show of high-handedness if they are to be successful, but Frazer had set about the unlawful requisitioning in a nervous and diffident fashion, having even gone so far as to track the flat's owner down, and persuade him to accept a small rent. He was afraid that in doing so he had aroused the man's suspicion. The happy couple were now comfortably installed, but Frazer admitted that every time there was a knock on the door his heart missed a beat, and he fully expected to find someone from the Provost Marshal's department waiting there when he went to open it.

Now they were engaged, Lola insisted on public recognition of her status. He had to give a party for Italians – most of them, he learned, big names on the black market, or minor Fascist officials she had known through her ex-lover. Worse, there had to be a party, too, for his brother officers. Frazer got out of inviting his CO, but the Adjutant had to be there, an officer who detested all foreigners – Italians in particular – and had himself disinfected before and after the occasion. The *pièce de résistance* of this celebration, which had been only sporadically gay, was a monster cake in the form of a heart, inscribed in icing sugar with their names, and more icing sugar, vermilion this time, to represent blood, cascading from it. She had also compelled him to show himself with her in the *Struscio*, the famous Easter-day parade in the Via Roma in which by a tradition, the origins of which are forgotten, all the participants drag their feet as they walk. To be seen in the company of a woman on this occasion is a statement of serious commitment. Once again he complained of aspects of their intimate relationship, mentioning that certain things were expected of him that he was unable to enthuse about. 'I seem to suffer from heartburn,' he said, 'but I'm sure it's only psychological.' I was able to help his morale by assuring him that even if Lola drove him to apply for permission to marry her, I had reason to know that there was very little chance that this would be granted.

April 25

After making mention of his new flat Frazer must have felt obliged to invite me round, because Lola appeared today with an invitation to dine with them tonight. The other guest proved to be the irrepressible Signorina Susanna, and she and Lola, glittering in party dresses and laden with ornaments, filled the bare environment of the flat with their chatter and laughter. The appointments of the flat were largely makeshift. It had been looted of all the furniture that could easily be carried away, and we sat on stools provided by the RASC at a very large and ornate table, which had been too cumbersome to steal. All the windows had been cracked in the bad raid of March 14, and brown paper stuck over the cracks with dismal effect.

Frazer gave an account of the engagement party, which sounded disastrous. Thinking it unwise to serve food that had obviously been stolen from army rations, Lola had done what she could on the basis of the black market. Thus, in addition to the famous cake, the guests had been served a spiced-up mess of egg-plant and tripe, which, delicious as it undoubtedly was, had not found favour with Frazer's brother officers. One, a lieutenant, had made a polite effort with a mouthful or two, but the Adjutant had simply let out a howl of dismay and pushed his plate away. From that moment the party seemed to have fallen apart. The officers had brought their whisky along, and soon the Adjutant was aggressively tight, to the point of blaming the girls for Mussolini's Abyssinian adventure, and putting on a little pantomime in description of Italian troops running away in battle. For this Susanna had called him a *cornuto* and a *stronzo*, neither of which expression he understood, although he must have guessed from the accompanying gestures that they were intended to be insulting. She then left the table followed by the lieutenant, inflamed by lust, who tried to corner her in the kitchen, and had his nose scratched for his pains.

For the present occasion Frazer had been able to steal a magnificent joint of beef – spoiled for him by the fact that Lola had punctured it in numerous places and thrust pieces of garlic into the holes. From the girls' point of view this was a banquet : army bacon eaten raw as an *hors d'œuvre*, beef bloodily succulent and fiery with garlic, and sweets from American K ration packs – so despised by the Americans, and so adored by everyone else. We were in the kitchen washing up after this feast when I smelt the smoke from the mobile smoke-screen units, and my heart sank, knowing that we were in for another raid. In a moment the others, too, realized what was happening, as the room filled with smoke, and we began to cough.

A shelter was provided for the use of tenants of the flats, which Frazer and I were reluctant to use for reasons of face. However, the girls refused to go unless we went with them, but before we could make up our minds the bombs started to come down. This raid was for me the worst of the war up till now. We grabbed the girls, pulled them away from the window, then stood in a row with our backs pressed to the wall. The windows blew in, the blackout screens flapping like enormous bats across the room, the ceiling in the dining-room came down in a gush of powder and slabs of plaster across the grand table, and the whole building began to heave and sway as if in the tremors of a moderate earthquake. Through the windows we saw the tracer-fire smudgily through pink smoke. By this time our hair, skins and clothing were coated with lime-dust. No one spoke, and neither girl showed any sign of fear.

The distant bombs came with a whistle that started high up in the sky, but the last one arrived silently, then deafened us. I felt the rise and fall of the building, and the cracking of walls; then hearing returned, first with the tinkle of falling shrapnel all round, and then, after an absolute silence, with a long, slow, deliberate rumble as the house next door collapsed.

That was the end of the raid. The all-clear sounded and we went down into the street. I found we were all chattering loudly in a childish and pointless fashion. The house next door was flattened into a double-decker sandwich of compressed floors, but I believe that no one was living there. Farther along the road in a clearing in the smoke we saw a building tilted like a sinking ship, and farther on still, a jeep blown into the air, hung by its front wheels from a roof rampart. The sight made us laugh.

Normally I detest night-clubs, but this seemed to be one occasion when it was absolutely necessary to go somewhere and dance. We found a place in Piedigrotto where they had a barrel-organ that only played four tunes, but that was enough, and we spent the rest of the evening there.

May 1

Today the arrival of summer was announced by the cry of the seller of venetian blinds – sad to the point of anguish in our narrow street – *s'e 'nfucato 'o sole* (the sun's turned fiery). Immediately, as if in response to a signal all Naples had awaited, the tempo of life changed and slowed down. As the melancholy howl was heard, first in the distance, then coming closer, people seemed to move cautiously into the shade, and those who hadn't already let down their blinds did so. Fans came out, girls walked about shading their eyes, and the seller of black-market cigarettes immediately under our window unfolded a Communist newspaper and held it over his head. We are told that after today stray dogs are liable to be picked up by the municipal catchers and knocked over the head.

Whitsun draws near – the Easter of the Roses, as they call it in Naples. On Saturday the general hope and expectation is that the blood of San Gennaro will liquefy in a satisfactory manner. It is believed by Neapolitans of all political creeds and degrees of religious conviction that the fortunes of the city depend on this phenomenon, and many advertisements have appeared in the newspapers paid for by commercial firms or political parties wishing the community 'a good and prosperous miracle'. A good miracle is one in which the blood liquefies quickly. A slow liquefaction is considered an ill omen for the ensuing year, while the complete failure of the miracle, which has rarely happened, is taken as a sign of the Saint's extreme displeasure, and regarded as a catastrophe.

It appears now that the Whitsun pilgrimage to Monte Vergine has definitely been vetoed, and this is a source of great public disappointment, and some criticism. This pilgrimage to the ancient shrine of Cybele, near Avellino, has been going on for six hundred years, since a miraculous picture of the Virgin was presented to the shrine by Catherine of Valois, and it is seen by the 50,000 or more devotees of this cult as dangerous to cancel an institution of this magnitude and spiritual value merely because there's a war on. Normally in these days the pilgrims travel by car to Avellino, after which the most devoted among them trudge the remaining few miles barefoot, up to the shrine. They then crawl on hands and knees from the sanctuary door to the altar. Religious duties at an end, somewhat bacchanalian picnics take place, followed by the singing of improvised songs on topical subjects. These, in an atmosphere of religious and alcoholic frenzy, frequently provoke quarrels, and the offended parties traditionally go behind the church, to settle their grievances, knife in hand, on the spot.

The public frustration over the pilgrimage was made much of by Lattarullo, who said that, among others, his aunt was very upset. Never having seen this aunt, who is supposed to live with him, or noticed the slightest sign of her presence in his flat, I am beginning to suspect she doesn't exist, and that he uses this fictitious personality as a showcase for all these Neapolitan prejudices of which he pretends to be ashamed.

Apart from Vittorio Emanuele's salver, the only object in Lattarullo's flat by which he sets any store is a large and dingy-looking piece of rock, which when first showing me he handled with the most reverent care. This was a souvenir from the cave-sanctuary of St Michael at Monte Santangelo, and of course, it belonged not to him, but to his mysterious aunt. Lattarullo is a highly educated man, with a cosmopolitan outlook and a wide grasp of world affairs, who reads everything he can lay his hands on including fifteen or twenty newspapers a day – three or four days out of date when he buys them – which can be picked up at the vegetable market for two or three lire a bundle. It is difficult for a man of his intellectual calibre to admit to me that he believes that San Gennaro can stop the flow of lava from Vesuvius, or that a monk in Pomigliano is flying about like a bird, so he gets round it by saying, 'My dear old aunt believes in this kind of thing. I don't want to argue with her. I only report these things to you to give you some idea of the mentality you're dealing with. As in the case of this Monte Vergine affair, I feel you should know. Mass hypnosis? I agree with you. You may well be right. But you have to remember that more people in this town share my aunt's point of view than mine.'

May 3

The Robin Hood tradition is strong in the Zona di Camorra, as it probably is in bandit country everywhere, an outstanding example of the breed being Domenico Lupo of Frattamaggiore, whose name, meaning wolf, has probably been an aid to his profession hitherto. Lupo, young, handsome and dashing, robber of the rich and a giver to the poor, was serving a stretch for banditry in a prison south of Rome. From this he was released by the advancing Allied troops, who as a matter of habit always loot the post offices and fling wide the prison gates in the territory they occupy. Lupo immediately headed south to reorganize his following. The officer who released him, greatly moved by his account of the political victimization he had undergone during the Mussolini regime, gave him a pass allowing him to travel anywhere he liked and a letter of recommendation describing his valued support of the Allied cause. Lupo produced the letter at the Naples headquarters of AMG to obtain more solid accreditation plus an AMG sticker for the windscreen of his stolen car. In the Zona di Camorra, teeming with criminals of every description, he began the recruitment of his new band and, making full use of his AMG pass, journeys were made in convoys of stolen cars to the battle areas, where an assortment of abandoned small arms, machine-guns, mortars, etc., were collected from the battle-field. Somewhere near the front line on the occasion of his last visit, Lupo claimed to have been received by an American divisional general, who listened to the story of his struggle against Fascism, presented him with several bottles of whisky, a pearl-handled pistol, and a religious picture from a ruined church.

Back in the Zona, Lupo settled down to prey on the cara-vans of the black market that followed the liberating armies in search of such scarce and sought-after commodities as teats for babies' bottles, cloth, nails and watches, which back in Naples fetched anything from ten to one hundred times their cost price. From this the Lupo band graduated to attacks on trains carrying military supplies northwards through Casoria to Caserta and to the battlefronts. In several cases, trains hijacked in this way, and usually defended by no more than a half-dozen guards, were completely emptied of their contents. In one instance, near Casoria, Lupo's band fought a victorious battle in which machine-guns and hand-grenades were used against a rival team, for the right to loot a train which they had held up.

At this point something obviously had to be done. Lupo's strength lay in the sympathy he had taken care to cultivate among the local peasantry; his well-publicized habit of descending on some poor family or deserving widow with a handful of thousand-lire notes or a sack of stolen food, and the romantic legend of his exploits as a womanizer. His weak-nesses stemmed from the fact that he was brash, vain, and foolhardy, without connections in the Camorra, who despise bandits however much they use them; that his men had killed policemen; finally that he had overstepped the mark even with the Allies by his attacks on trains.

His downfall was organized by a temporary combination of all the police forces in the area, and for once the Carabinieri and the Pubblica Sicurezza came together to suspend their mutual detestation, pool their information, and work out a plan of attack. One of the Carabinieri marshals, it was explained to me by Marshal Lo Scalzo of Caivano, had put forward a scheme for exploiting the natural breach opened in Lupo's defences by his pose of the lover of many women. The bandit made a great thing of having a girl in every town in the area, but he also had a regular mistress who was notoriously jealous. Whenever Lupo was in the Caivano district it was believed that this girl slipped away to spend the night with him, but nobody had been able to discover where the couple met. However, the girl had now been approached, and the softening-up process expected to lead to a final betrayal had been begun by showing her photographs taken of Lupo in the company of other females. As the bandit had a passion for being photographed, some of these were genuine enough. Others were clever fakes, and I was shown one which – through some dexterous photo-montage – showed Lupo with his arms and legs twined round a naked prostitute. The Neapolitan police stopped at nothing. I saw a picture of the mistress involved, too, who looked like a glum version of Carmen Miranda, with a sour expression, and a turned-down, pouting mouth.

These dingy professional secrets came to me in the hope that I would report back favourably on the police's determination and zeal, as a result of which none of the General's terrible threats of demotion or even prosecution could be carried out. Marshal Lo Scalzo said at the time the plot was disclosed, that it was no longer a question whether Lupo would be taken, but when. He was also particularly anxious that I should be in at the kill, and see that, after all, the Carabinieri were a match for the reputedly invincible Lupo. This evening a young policeman from Caivano turned up at the Riviera di Chiaia asking me to be at the police station there by dawn.

I left the HQ at about four this morning, taking the Match-

less, and was in Caivano in half an hour, with the sun still
not up. It was amazing to see the activity on the roads once
outside the limits of the town: peasants in their hundreds,
hooded in the half-light, kicking up the dust as they trudged
along on the way to their fields. Some of them were singing
African-sounding songs, very different from the soft, sugary
melodies of the Neapolitans of the city.

At Caivano I found a gathering of both kinds of police,
some of them with the faces of men, and some of devils. The
Carabinieri station was full of gusty, sinister laughter, and
jokes about death, while a distribution was made of obsolete
guns, and the fearsome and fickle *diavolo-rosso* hand-grenades
used by the Italian army. We then bundled into two crumpled
old Fiats, and were on our way. To avoid the possibility of
Lupo's being warned by his spies that we were coming, we left
Caivano heading for Afragola in the opposite direction, then
swung in an arc through a landscape as flat as Holland towards
the farmhouse off the Frattamaggiore road where the final
treason had been prepared and the lovers, it was to be hoped,
were still peacefully sleeping.

This was a landscape that favoured concealment. Every field
was surrounded by tall fruit-trees, and these were linked
together by the runners of the enormous and ancient vines to
which each tree in local parlance was 'married'; their branches
carried along parallel wires, one above the other, to form a
hedge, or enclosure, about fifteen feet in height.

The farmhouse that was our target was in the middle of
such a vine-enclosed field; a grey cube barely visible through
the foliage, and here a police spy waited in hiding to assure
us that all was well and no one had left the house. We left the
cars under the screen of the vines, and set out to the attack.
The maize was up to our chests but we were in view of the
single window in the grey wall, and the *Commissario* in his
city suit, panting and snorting at my side, held a grenade in
his hand ready to deal with the window. Half the party had
gone off to take the house from the rear. A wolf-hound came

out, and then ran off when somebody pointed a gun at it. A Carabiniere started to kick in the door, and we heard a single shot and a great shouting from the back of the house.

Here we found Lupo lying on the ground. He was dressed only in a shirt, and had jumped from the bedroom window at the back, breaking a leg, and – from the state of his face – had almost certainly received a swipe from a rifle butt. One eye was closing and the other looked up at us unblinkingly. Blood from mouth and nose had filled in the deep lines of his face, and his expression was impassive.

Moments later a woman was hustled into sight by one of the Carabinieri. She was barefoot, in rumpled clothes, dull and dazed-looking and plain to the point of ugliness.

'The woman in the case,' Lo Scalzo said.

'They're rather rough with her, aren't they?' I said.

'She let her man down. They don't like that kind of thing.'

'But she's been working for you.'

'It doesn't mean we have to like her.'

'What will happen to them now?'

'He'll go down for life, and one of his brothers will kill her. They'll soon find out she threw him in. A knife up through the vagina into the belly. Or a red-hot poker if they have time. She'll be dead within the year.'

May 7

Despite gloomy forecasts, the blood of San Gennaro liquefied successfully yesterday evening. The miracle took place in a slow and reluctant manner. By tradition this is seen as a poor omen for the coming year, with the result that the Neapolitans are left with a feeling hardly better than gloomy relief. It is fantastic to realize that outright failure could have produced a security crisis, and that we should certainly have had large-scale civil commotions on our hands.

Crowds had been beginning to form in the neighbourhood of the Duomo since Friday evening, and one immediately noticed their heavy silence. By Saturday afternoon some agitation and local pockets of hysteria were evident. The popular feeling was one of nervous listlessness coupled with apprehension. All the fishing-boats were in port and the shops and cafés were empty. People simply mooched about the streets, waiting. It was like a weird parody of a public holiday. The two women who work for us got through their chores as fast as they could and went off to light candles in our local shrine in the Vico Freddo. Lattarullo put the feelings of educated middle-class Neapolitans into words : 'Much as I deplore the fact that living in the twentieth century we should be so obsessed by these relics of medievalism, I'm afraid that even I am not immune to mass suggestion.'

At about 5 p.m. a disturbance started in the narrow streets at the rear of the Duomo, a few shop-windows were broken, and MPs moved into the area in strength. An hour later I found it impossible to get through the Strada di Tribunali. People were running hither and thither, entranced and ecstatic, frothing at the mouth and prophesying doom. It was like being caught up in a wild football crowd, frenzied by the prospect of their side's impending defeat. A hubbub was said to have started in the Cathedral because a number of British and American officers had been allotted seats close to the altar, and the crowd suspected that their presence might be holding up the miracle. There were cries of 'Out with the heretics,' which may not have been understood by the military guests, although some of them must have noticed the fists waved in their direction.

Soon after this the *Parenti di San Gennaro* were led in to take up their position round the altar. These aged women are popularly credited with being actual descendants of the Saint, and they form a mysterious and spiritually potent clique, who have inherited power and the responsibility of browbeating their ancestor into submission with threats and curses, when all else fails.

At about 8 p.m. the Saint gave way to this new pressure

and the miracle took place. Some public jubilation followed, but on a muted scale, and most people just went home to bed. A poorish liquefaction but better than none at all, was the general verdict. We shall have to go through this all over again in September.

May 7

A shameful example of the perfidiousness and injustices of this war we conduct behind the scenes. The General has not been able to get over the episode of the two rival bands fighting a battle for the right to pillage one of our trains, nor has he been mollified by the news of the capture of the bandit Lupo. One man is not enough. He wants mass arrests, and yesterday all the Italian chiefs of police were called before him and threatened with every kind of sanction including charges of sabotage if they failed to produce immediate results. The police chiefs are said to have replied that their forces were grossly under-manned, and their hands tied by excessive scruples shown by the Allies in the matter of repression. Only if given a free hand to solve this problem in their own way could results be guaranteed. Thus today I took part as an observer in one of the new-style operations : a raid on a bandit hideout carried out by a mixed force of Carabinieri and Pubblica Sicurezza, under orders to get results at all costs.

This time the combined force numbered about 50 men, but included the same Carabinieri as at Frattamaggiore and the same hyena-faced Pubblica Sicurezza Commissario, with his pin-striped suit, red-devil hand-grenades and squeaking shoes. The fields we moved into in a wide then gradually tightening circle were as before, fenced in by their enormous vines, with little grey cubes of houses, and occasional straw-shelters where the peasants kept their tools and took a nap in the shade in the worst of the noonday sun. In one of these four armed men were discovered. They immediately surrendered, were hand-cuffed, chained together and led away. But now a problem presented itself. Only four prisoners had been taken, and a man could be charged with banditry only if he was a member of a criminal association of not less than five persons. As it was, the four captured men, who by legal definition were not bandits, could have applied for bail, with the near-certainty of getting it. In this country there are fifty lawyers to every one policeman, and the lawyers expect to win. But a bandit gets no bail and faces a sentence of from five to thirty years.

The solution in this case was to go straight to the nearest village to the house of a man who happened to have a criminal record and arrest him. He became the essential fifth bandit. His resignation was astonishing. He kissed his family goodbye, allowed himself to be chained up without protest and was led off. Solitary confinement in the iron womb of Poggio Reale awaited him. Then a long, slow wasting away of body and mind on the island of Procida, of which little but blood-chilling legends was known. When, if ever, he returned to his village he would find his children gone and his wife grown old. How much better it would have been, how much more humane, simply to have shot all five 'while attempting to escape'.

May 9

The impudence of the black market takes one's breath away. For months now official sources have assured us that the equivalent of the cargo of one Allied ship in three unloaded in the Port of Naples is stolen. The latest story going the rounds is that when a really big-scale coup is planned and it is necessary to clear the port to handle bulky goods, someone arranges for the air-raid sirens to sound and for the mobile smoke-screens to provide their fog, under the cover of which the shock-troops of the black market move in to do their work.

Stolen equipment sold on the Via Forcella, and round the law courts – where one-man-business thieves without protection are tried and sentenced by the dozen every day for possession of Allied goods – is now on blatant display, tastefully arranged with coloured ribbon, a vase of flowers, neatly-written showcards advertising the quality of the looted goods. COMPARE OUR PRICES . . . WARRANTED PURE AUSTRALIAN WOOL . . . MONEY BACK IF FOUND TO SHRINK . . . YOU CAN MARCH TO KINGDOM COME ON THESE BEAUTIFUL IMPORTED BOOTS . . . IF YOU DON'T SEE THE OVERSEAS ARTICLE YOU'RE LOOKING FOR, JUST ASK US AND WE'LL GET IT. Tailors all over Naples are taking uniforms to pieces, dying the material, and turning them into smart new outfits for civilian wear. I hear that even British Army long-coms, which despite the climate still find their way over here, are accepted with delight, dyed red, and turned into the latest thing in track suits.

In the first days the MPs carried out a few half-hearted raids on the people specializing in these adaptations, but they found too many smart new overcoats made from Canadian blankets awaiting collection by Italian friends of General this and Colonel that to be able to put a stop to the thing. Last week the Papal Legate's car, held up by pure accident in some routine road-check, was found to be fitted with a set of stolen tyres. Many apologies and smiles and His Reverence was waved on. Other than commando daggers and bayonets, they don't display looted weapons in the stalls, but the advice from my contacts is that there is no problem except the cash in arranging to buy anything from a machine-gun to a light tank.

The trouble now is that certain items which can be freely and easily bought on the black market are in short supply in the Army itself. This applies currently to photographic equipment and materials, practically all of which has been stolen to be sold under the counter in shops in the Via Roma, and to certain medical supplies, in particular penicillin. Every sick civilian can go to a pharmacist and get a course of penicillin injections at a time when supplies in the military hospitals are about to run out. At last the time has come when the effect of the black market on the war effort has become evident. It could have been wiped out, but because of the secret involvement in it through their Italian connections of some of our high authorities, it was not. Now, the decision has been reached that something will have to be done. It is too late now to abolish the black market, but at least an attempt will be made to tidy it up. Probably for this reason I was called on today by the FSO and ordered to investigate the penicillin racket.

The first move was to visit the pharmacist Casana with whom we have been on excellent terms, and to ask him in the strictest confidence where his penicillin came from. Casana a little shocked, but resigned, supplied the name Vittorio Fortuna, living in the Via dei Mille, but warned me that if he was called as a witness against this man he would probably lose his life. I checked this name with other pharmacists, all of whom knew of Fortuna and agreed that he was known to deal in penicillin, although they all denied any connection with him. Fortuna, they agreed, was under the protection of someone in Allied Military Government. Having heard this, I decided that my best course was to go to the American Counter-Intelligence Corps, who are well in with AMG, whereas we are not.

Although we and the CIC perform roughly the same function in Naples, and they have recently moved into the floor above us in the same building, there has never been any official contact between us. Currently their strength is about 25 agents and one officer. Those who have been lucky enough to glimpse it say they have the finest filing system in all Italy, but they are handicapped by the fact that not a single one of them speaks a word of Italian, which makes them wholly dependent upon an interpreter who once featured on our list of suspects. The organizations, often working separately and without any exchange of information on the same cases, constantly overlap and sometimes come into conflict, so that with fair frequency we lock up each other's friends, and spring each other's suspects, treading on each other's toes with what might be described as good-humoured tolerance.

Our only collaboration with the CIC has been the agreement by which we borrow their jeeps for holiday jaunts in return for a bottle of whisky, which inexplicably is the only thing any American soldier could possibly desire for his pleasure or comfort that the PX does not supply. My whisky-for-jeep arrangement is with Special Agent Frank Edwards, and I discussed the matter of Fortuna with him.

Edwards said that it was well known in the CIC that Fortuna was a lieutenant of Vito Genovese, and he gave me a thumbnail sketch of Genovese's history. Genovese, according to Edwards, was not, as described on our files, ex-secretary to Al Capone, nor was he even a Sicilian, but had been born in the village of Ricigliano, near Potenza. He had been second-in-command of a New York Mafia 'family' headed by Lucky Luciano, Edwards said, and had succeeded to its leadership when Luciano was gaoled, after which he had been acknowledged as the head of all the American Mafia. Shortly before the outbreak of war Genovese had returned to Italy to escape a murder indictment in the US, had become a friend of Mussolini's, and then, with the Duce's fall, transferred his allegiance to Allied Military Government, where he was now seen as the power behind the scenes. Genovese controlled the sindacos in most towns within fifty miles of Naples. He leased out rackets to his followers, took a toll of everything, threw crumbs of favour to those who kept in step with him, and found a way of punishing opposition.

What was to be done? Nothing, Edwards said. The CIC had soon learned to steer clear of any racket in which Genovese had a finger – and his finger was in most. Too many American officers had been chosen to go on the Italian campaign because they were of Italian descent. For this reason it was hoped they might easily adapt to the environment, and this they had done all too well. The American-Italians in AMG reigned supreme and knew how to close their ranks when threatened from without. An American CID agent who had cottoned on to the fact that the notorious Genovese was in virtual control in Naples and set out to investigate his present activities, soon found himself isolated and powerless, and all the reward he had had for his pains was loss of promotion. And would this situation apply in his opinion in the case of any Briton who threatened Genovese's interests? Edwards didn't know, and suggested I might go ahead and try. He would be most interested to see what happened.

The Allied Military Proclamation, in one or another of its many clauses, seems to authorize one to do almost anything to anybody who, to use the proclamation's own words, 'does any act to the prejudice of the good order, safety or security of the Allied Forces', and I put a copy of the proclamation into my pocket before going to see Fortuna. He was a calm, handsome man, with a religious medal dangling in the opening of his shirt, a controlled but charming smile, and a strange primness of manner, which came out in the exclamation *'Mamma mia!'* when I explained the reason for my call. He irritated me by addressing me as if I were a child, using verbs in the infinitive and speaking with exaggerated slowness and clarity. I showed him the proclamation and told him I was going to search his flat, and he smiled and shrugged his shoulders and invited me to go ahead. The search took a full hour. I worked my way methodically through the rooms, and in doing so discovered nothing more than the normal range of black-market goods that one would expect to find in any flat of this kind. I probed and poked into every corner, examined floorboards, tapped on walls, checked the cistern, dismantled a big old-fashioned gas-heater, and at last in a waste-paper basket under the kitchen sink, found an empty carton that had contained penicillin and with it one damaged phial.

Showing Fortuna the penicillin I told him I was going to arrest him and, still perfectly relaxed and agreeable, he said, 'This will do you no good. Who are you? You are no one. I was dining with a certain colonel last night. If you are tired of life in Naples, I can have you sent away.'

On the way to Poggio Reale his mood never changed, and he became chatty and affable. Would they cut his hair off and make him wear prison uniform? I told him they wouldn't until he'd been tried, found guilty and sentenced. When was I going to question him? To this I replied, as soon as I could find the time, but that there might be some little delay, owing to pressure of work. And in the meanwhile? he asked. In the meanwhile, I told him, he'd stay in Poggio Reale where he'd be out of harm's way. I handed him over to the half-crazy turnkeys, who fingerprinted him and signed him in, and told him I'd see him in two or three days. He laughed, and said, 'You won't find me here when you come back.'

May 11

To Poggio Reale to see Fortuna, whom I found dapper and imperturbable as ever. He was busy with what looked like an excellent meal specially brought in, and courteously invited me to join him. He gave me the impression of a man buoyed up with secret knowledge of the way his future was likely to go. I told him that I was so hard pressed for time that I could only spare ten minutes, and that if he felt that there was anything he should say, now was his chance, because I was not sure how long it would be before I could get back again. He asked me what I wanted of him and I told him all the details of the racket in penicillin, including the names of those concerned, and in particular those employed by AMG. Any co-operation he could give in this way would be taken into account at his trial. Fortuna said, 'Whatever I tell you or don't tell you makes no difference. I'll be acquitted.'

This, as I had to agree inwardly, was a strong possibility. We had filled the prison with little men like the half-crazed Antonio Priore who had been sentenced to long terms of imprisonment for petty crimes, but every single one of the big fish, Signorini, De Amicis, Del Blasio, Castronuovo, and the rest of them had got off scot-free. Witnesses had disappeared

or they had retracted their evidence. They had perjured themselves in court, and gone cheerfully to prison as a result of
their perjury. Repeatedly the prosecution had bungled its case
and whether by accident or design essential documents had
constantly been lost. We knew through our informants of at
least one case in which one of our judges had been offered, at
a dinner-party, a huge sum to see to it that a man up for trial
was cleared. Whether or not he accepted it we should never
know, but the defendant was found not guilty. All such powerful and well-connected defendants were found not guilty, while
the cells of Poggio Reale and Procida were crowded with
small-time receivers and thieves who would rot away in them
for the rest of their useful lives. Justice was never seen to be
done; and if ever there was a place where it was on sale, it
was Naples. If the defence could afford to employ Lelio
Porzio, the finest criminal lawyer in Italy, acquittal was certain. In defending one client he delivered a speech lasting
2½ days, in which Browning and Shakespeare were quoted,
and the proceedings at one point were held up to allow the
judge and jury to regain emotional control. It cost a fortune
to retain Porzio but in our experience he had never been
known to lose a case.

There was no doubt that Porzio would defend Fortuna,
too, if the case could ever be brought to court, and that so far
I had no firm witnesses, although I hoped to get one. What
was needed was a little time, and in the meanwhile it seemed
essential to keep Fortuna in a place where he would be at
least hampered in his efforts to bend the law to his will,
intimidate all possible witnesses, and call his friends in AMG
to his aid. To undermine his unshattered belief that he would
be rescued in a matter of days, I mentioned in anecdotal
fashion, but with perfect truth, that such was the chronic
muddle in the administration of the gaol that prisoners actually
got lost, and cited a case – through a mix-up over names –
where two detainees had been called for in the night, put on
a boat in the port and shipped off to Tripoli in the belief that

they had escaped from gaol there. This information was intended to convey a hint that it was always possible that something of the kind could happen to him, Fortuna. But I knew it couldn't, and that Fortuna was not the kind of man to allow himself to be victimized by a bureaucratic blunder. I was trying a little bluff, without too much hope of success. Fortuna was accustomed to dealing with men with far-reaching and mysterious powers, and I hoped that he might be encouraged in the fallacy that I possessed them too, and for this reason might be inclined to come to terms. He seemed impressed, but still had nothing useful to say, so I told him I hoped to be back in a week and went off to see Casana again.

Nothing would induce Casana to change his mind not to give evidence against Fortuna – this much I expected, but he said he had heard of someone who probably would for a consideration, a certain Dr Lanza who was a business rival of Fortuna's. Casana couldn't approve of Lanza, who he mentioned was from the North, and therefore completely indifferent to matters of honour.

I found Dr Lanza in his clinic, which smelt not only of ether but success. He had a fine Lancia car outside with an AMG sticker on the windscreen, and he showed me affectionate letters and recommendations from half a dozen colonels, and passes enabling him to go anywhere within reason. The doctor had an absolutely frank and straightforward proposition to make. In exchange for giving evidence against Fortuna, who had sold him penicillin he only subsequently found out to have been stolen, he asked for a solemn promise that a way would be found of getting him to Rome as soon as it fell. Lanza admitted, as if to an act of Christian charity, that his motive for the trip would be to fill his car with pharmaceutical and other products bought at prices as low as one-fiftieth of those currently paid in Naples. I told him that such a deal might be considered. It seemed a low price to pay for the certainty – because it was unlikely that Lanza could be made to disappear, or retract his evidence – of a victory over the black market.

Back to Poggio Reale in the hope that Fortuna might have weakened. I was by now certain that Lanza would give evidence, and would be an excellent witness, having discovered that there was an additional motive to the commercial one in the form of a long-standing feud between the two men. For all this, optimism was waning. I was reminded of the ominous fact that at our last interview I had found Fortuna in a cell by himself, although such was the prison overcrowding that up to six, even occasionally eight, men were put into a cell together. His cell had looked well kept, which suggested to me that he paid another prisoner to look after it. In fact he was being treated as a privileged person. Anything could happen in a place like Poggio Reale. It was a mysterious world of which we knew nothing with certainty, but of which we heard the most astonishing rumours. One heard of prisoners whose names were on the register spending weekends in Capri, and of the aristocrats of the underworld – of which Fortuna would be one – giving champagne parties in their cells on their saints' days for their cronies and the ladies of the town; of family visits and the usual exchange of gifts at Christmas and the Epiphany and Easter. If it is a fact that in Naples everything is for sale, how much more true must this be in Poggio Reale?

A message waited at the *Ufficio Matricola* to say the Governor wanted to see me. When I went to his office I saw the American master-sergeant, supposed to have been dismissed as adviser to the Governor for selling prison equipment. He was sitting in the anteroom, and he looked up from the comic book he was reading, waved and smiled, and I went in. It turned out that the Governor himself was away sick. His deputy, a small, dried-out, light-starved functionary, sighed deeply before pushing a doctor's certificate across the desk. This said that Fortuna was suffering from appendicitis with grave complications, and as the facilities for his treatment were not available in the prison, he had had to be moved out to a civilian hospital.

The Deputy Governor's eyes met mine and he cupped the tips of the fingers of his right hand and allowed it to oscillate slowly from the wrist. The gesture meant 'what do you expect? This is Naples. These are the facts of life.'

What was to be done? I was absolutely certain that I could take a doctor with me to this hospital where we should find Fortuna with an incision in the abdomen. We should be told that he had been operated upon for the removal of the appendix – and he quite possibly had. Ways and means would be found to see to it that he was running a temperature by the time we were admitted. We should be told that recovery would be slow, and convalescence long. After that the ball would be in my court. I could insist on taking him back to Poggio Reale, where the hospital facilities would certainly be primitive, but it would look like victimization to anyone who did not know the inside facts of the case, and Fortuna would have some justification for an appeal to AMG, who would be certain to refer the matter to No. 3 District.

When I reported all these facts and these dispiriting probabilities to the FSO and asked if I should go ahead, he said, 'I simply don't see how you can spare the time,' and that just about summed the matter up.

May 28

The French colonial troops are on the rampage again. Whenever they take a town or a village, a wholesale rape of the population takes place. Recently all females in the villages of Patricia, Pofi, Isoletta, Supino, and Morolo were violated. In Lenola, which fell to the Allies on May 21, fifty women were raped, but – as these were not enough to go round – children and even old men were violated. It is reported to be normal for two Moroccans to assault a woman simultaneously, one having normal intercourse while the other commits sodomy.

In many cases severe damage to the genitals, rectum and uterus has been caused. In Castro di Volsci doctors treated 300 victims of rape, and at Ceccano the British have been forced to build a guarded camp to protect the Italian women. Many Moors have deserted, and are attacking villages far behind the lines, and now they are reported to have appeared in the vicinity of Afragola to add a new dimension of terror to that already produced by the presence of so many marauders.

Today I went to Santa Maria a Vico to see a girl said to have been driven insane as the result of an attack by a large party of Moors. I found her living alone with her mother (who had also been raped a number of times), and in total poverty. Her condition had improved, and she behaved rationally and with a good deal of charm, although she was unable to walk as the result of physical injuries. The Carabinieri and the PS said that she had been certified as insane, and would have been committed to an asylum had a bed been available. She would be unlikely in the circumstances ever to find a husband.

At last one had faced the flesh-and-blood reality of the kind of horror that drove the whole female population of Macedonian villages to throw themselves from cliffs rather than fall into the hands of the advancing Turks. A fate worse than death : it was in fact just that.

Back at the Municipio I was confronted by a group of sindacos from neighbouring towns, and an ultimatum was presented : 'Either clear the Moroccans out, or we will deal with them in our own way.' All these men looked like the toughest of movie gangsters, and I was convinced they would carry out their threat.

What is it that turns an ordinary decent Moroccan peasant boy into the most terrible of sexual psychopaths as soon as he becomes a soldier? From further enquiries among the communities that have suffered from them I learned that the attackers of the Santa Maria a Vico family were roaming the countryside in several jeeps, led by a sergeant-chef who fancied himself as a dancer, and dressed up as a female when not in action.

May 31

The fragmentation of Italian politics in reaction to the long stagnant acquiescence under Fascism continues. There are now some sixty officially recognized political parties having memberships ranging from a hundred or so to nearly two million. Many of these offer bizarre recipes for national salvation, including a small band of fanatics in the Salerno area who claim to have discovered the solution of the problem of perpetual motion, and to be ready to exploit this in the national interest. In addition to the legally constituted parties there are clandestine Neo-Fascists, and Separatists. To the latter group I believe we have given secret support. The Separatists' latest plan for Italy's regeneration includes the immediate demolition of all factories, the abolition of the motor-car, and the renaming of the months of the calendar after the Roman gods. This is the season and situation when insanity has become almost respectable.

Of all the emergent political forces the most numerous, powerful and rational – outside Naples, in which the urban sub-proletariat is Royalist to a man – are the Christian Democrats, the Social Democrats, and the orthodox Communists; the last being somewhat sapped in strength by the existence of some thirty factional groups, each with its own news-sheet, all mutually hostile, and in agreement only in calling on the workers of the world to unite.

The odds are that when the elections come the Christian Democrats will take over power. This is the party of the Church as well as that of the great landlords, and it is supported by all the energy, the political finesse, and the devotion of the religious Establishment. Both the bosses and the Church are already putting on the pressure. Armies of nuns go from house to house in the working-class districts, explaining to wives what political democracy is all about, and why it will be sinful to vote for any party other than that of God and His angels. To support these spiritual pressures, there are other inducements. An unemployed man who is inscribed with the CD has more chance of finding a job than one who isn't, and the canvassing nuns often make small handouts of *pasta* or flour that necessitous families find it very hard to refuse.

In the absence abroad of Togliatti, the head of the orthodox Communist Party is Eugenio Reale. The party shows every sign, as soon as the liberation is complete, of being the strongest CP outside the Soviet Union. Unlike Communist Parties elsewhere, its membership contains a high proportion of middle-class intellectuals; some of them wealthy, and many with legal training. A powerful and dangerous political force.

I have known Reale for two months, and have visited him a half-dozen times in his flat in the Via Gravina. He is calm and softly-spoken, impressive in his analysis of the Italian political situation, and endowed with a belief hardly distinguishable from religious faith of the eventual takeover of power by the Communist Party. This he sees as happening after the Christian Democrats have held office and have provoked national disillusionment by a public display of corruption. Reale talks happily and confidently of these things to come. We are the best of friends, but there are the usual currents of self-interest in the friendship. Certain of our high-level strategists are obsessed with the importance of undercover Neo-Fascist groups, believing that should we ever suffer a military setback these people would come out of their holes and go into action as partisans for the Germans. As these people see it, nobody should be better placed than the leader of the Communists to know who these secret plotters are. Perhaps they are right, but all my visits to the Via Gravina have produced less useful information than a single meeting with, say, Lattarullo.

I suspect that Eugenio Reale knows precisely what I am

after, but is not in the slightest bit interested in supplying it. He is not afraid of Neo-Fascists. He is probably happy that they should exist, that the Separatists should exist, that the Party of Perpetual Motion should exist, and that the country should be politically divided and fissured in the way it is. I believe that it suits his book that his political enemies should tear themselves to pieces fighting each other, that the bosses should force their workers to join the Christian Democrats, that the nuns should go on handing out spaghetti, and that the professional clappers should be employed at 10 lire a head to applaud at meetings organized by the Christian Democrats, and howl down the speakers of their opponents. These people are sowing the wind and Reale is preparing the whirlwind they will reap. Political division and confusion are what his party thrives on, and more and more voters will eventually take refuge in the ironclad philosophy he provides.

In the meanwhile I press him for the names of secret Fascists, and to my astonishment at our meeting today he seemed to have given way. A piece of paper was put into my hand on which he had listed the names of the four most dangerous men in Naples, and that of a subversive newspaper to be suppressed. Alas, they turned out to be no more than Enrico Russo, leader of the Trotskyists, and his lieutenants Antonio Ceechi, Villone Libero and Luigi Balzano. Reale's 'Fascist News-sheet' was the left-wing Communist organ, *Il Proletario*. So much wasted effort. I should have known.

June 4

The inevitable has happened with the murder of five Moors in a village near Cancello. They were enticed into a house with the offer of women, and then given food or wine containing some paralysing poison. While fully conscious they were castrated, and then beheaded. The decapitation was entrusted to pubescent boys to prove their worth, but the boys lacked both the skill and strength to carry the task out in a speedy and effective manner. The bodies were buried under cabbages, which were first dug up and then replanted over them in several village gardens, and there has been an undercurrent of sinister merriment in the Zona di Camorra about the prospects of fine vegetable crops in the coming year. These facts were passed to me by my reliable contact in Afragola.

The Psychological Warfare Bureau has been very energetic in its investigations into the crimes committed by the Moors. I wonder if any news of this episode will find it way into the bulletin.

June 7

Called on Lattarullo whose fortunes have taken a turn for the better as a result of the fall of Rome last week. He can now play his part again at funerals as 'the uncle from Rome', and his first engagement, fixed through the agency for which he has worked in the past, is for this afternoon. Ideally he should be met at the Stazione Centrale and be seen to descend from a first-class carriage, but as the trains are not yet running this is impossible. Instead, the agency will supply a car fitted with Roman numbers, and a driver in an American semi-uniform of the kind that can be bought for a few thousand lire with whatever stripes and ribbons one feels like sporting, in the Via Forcella. The car will pick him up in the Piazza Dante, and deliver him right to the door.

It seemed remarkable to me that Lattarullo could hope to avoid recognition by any of the mourners as the local figure he was, but he seemed confident that this was unlikely to happen. For my benefit he put on the sleek, new, black suit and the black hat supplied by the agency, seeming to have stiffened and straightened in doing so. His face, too, seemed to have changed as part of the disguise, transformed by a solemnity that had affected even the bone-structure. He mentioned that Neapolitans as a race tended to live out their lives in the district where they had been born, which in effect were enormous separate villages, for which reason he would never accept a commission of this kind in his native Chiaia. For the rest, he studied the information supplied by the agency about the family background, and in his grief-stricken patrician aloofness kept apart from the rest of the guests. This was a species of solemn pantomime, he said, and he was sure that the mourners saw it that way too and were not inclined to pry into the details of the stage-management. He came on the scene looking like a Roman, he could put on a presentable Roman accent, he kept his hands to his sides, and snapped an answer to a question in the way a Roman was supposed to, and he was of the belief that most people were happy to settle for that. The fee for his services would be 2000 lire – an enormous windfall which he would accept with dignity and no fulsome show of gratitude. He expected that he would be urged to take home with him small gifts of pasta, a mozzarella cheese, and perhaps a little oil, and this he would do.

Other trivial deceptions had been arranged for this funeral, which was to take place in the Rione San Antonio Abate, an area which is obsessed by Neapolitan working-class display and the putting on of what is known as *una bella faccia*. The magnificent silk-lined coffin in which the corpse would be displayed would eventually be substituted by one of plain deal; even the flowers were on hire and would be collected when the last of the mourners had gone and made to serve for three or four more funerals. Neapolitans, said Lattarullo, had come to realize that there was not much point in leaving flowers in cemeteries, where raiders paid daily visits, collecting them for resale, and transforming wreaths into bridal bouquets.

While on the subject of Neapolitan villainy, he had news of a spectacular case reported this week from the Monte Vergine section, featuring a notorious woman black marketeer who had amassed four million lire' worth of gold and jewels and hidden them in the furniture of her house. Here she was visited by three distressed strangers in clerical garb, two of them holding up the third – a bishop, they said – who had just suffered a heart attack in the street. The chaplain and the major-domo, as they described themselves, carried the 'bishop' in and laid him on the woman's bed, while she stayed respectfully outside in the street waiting for him to recover. Half an hour or so later she decided to risk a peep through the door, and found that her visitors had left, having cleared out the house before their departure.

June 9

Into the 92nd General Hospital on Wednesday last, once again with malaria. Three days as usual of grinding headache and sickness, after which I felt reasonably well, and faced only the problem of persuading a highly sympathetic MO to let me out. Yesterday I explained to him the urgent nature of my duties and he agreed to allow contacts to visit me in hospital. Today Del Giudice and Lattarullo turned up in the morning, immediately followed by Lo Scalzo in the company of Donna Maria Fidora, the ex-python wrestler from Caivano, and a sincere but saturnine-looking member of the Camorra of Afragola. In the afternoon Lola and Susanna appeared, both in slave-jewellery and feathered head-dresses. Whatever the MO might have said, the ward sister, tight-lipped and muttering, did not approve. Screens were put round my bed while the visitors were present, and as soon as Lola and Susanna had gone the sister went away and came back with a medical major carrying a spray with which he proceeded to disinfect about a quarter of the ward in the vicinity of my bed.

The news is that Frazer has been posted – or has got himself posted – so his great affair with Lola has come to an end. Both girls will now retire to Ischia for the summer season, in their own words 'to deflate'. They explained to me that the part of the island facing Naples is radio-active, and iodine is wafted on the sea-breezes. The effect is slimming, and of special benefit, as well, to the kidneys, the bladder, and the complexion. As part of the cure they will feed on rabbits of a kind bred only on the island. These are reared in total darkness, and their pale, almost transparent, non-fattening flesh is a gastronomic feature of the regime.

Things having turned out this way, I imagine the ex-Federale will shortly be sending his wife into summer exile in a *pension* on Capri, to leave the field clear for visits to Ischia, and that as the noise of war recedes, he and Lola will achieve a cosy readjustment, assisted by *iniezioni recostituenti*. Unpleasant memories will be pushed into the background, and soon it will be as if nothing had ever come between them.

June 27

A week of fiestas, processions and miraculous happenings. Simmons of the Bari Section, spending a night with us, described a medieval spectacle he had watched at Guarda Sanframondi where an order of flagellants half-kill themselves every seven years in honour of their Virgin. This bloody display of fervour is frowned on by the Vatican and was suppressed under Fascism, when it was felt that such spectacles did little to support the image of Italy as a modern industrial nation. In the current atmosphere of disillusionment, escapism and hysteria, it has been resuscitated with enthusiasm. Several hundred hooded and white-robed penitents who had prepared themselves for the day by long periods of fasting and abstention from sexual intercourse practically took over the village and paraded through the streets, beating themselves on the bare chest with pieces of sharp rock. Simmons said their robes were soaked with blood. There was a dramatic moment when a man carrying one of the banners was publicly accused of being a cuckold – a crime by local standards. He was rescued from lynching by the police, and taken into protective custody.

Eric Williams has been telling us about his frustrations at Nola, where the whole life of the town came to a standstill last Sunday for the celebration of the Feast of the Lily, as a result of which the Military in general, and Signals in particular, are in something of a plight. For the *festa* eight enormously high wooden towers, the 'lilies', are built, and these, decorated with flowers, are carried through every street in honour of St Paulinus who in the fifth century invented church bells in this town. Unfortunately all the main army telephone connections between the North and the Far South, including Sicily, go through Nola, and wires and cables by the hundred were cut to allow the lilies to go through. The resulting chaos in communications, he said, was unimaginable.

On the self-same day that Eric was suffering in Nola, Del Giudice, who has become a useful contact, asked me if I would take him to Amalfi. He obviously preferred not to say why. Totting up the balance of favours, I decided he was in credit and, having a free day, did my usual deal with the Counter-Intelligence Corps for the loan of a jeep, and we drove there together.

Del Giudice, a great amateur of local gastronomy, wanted me to taste the eels which at this time of the year are a speciality of the town. We visited what he said was the best restaurant along that part of the coast but I did not really enjoy the meal. Sea-food restaurants always seem to me more prone to evident and visual cruelty than others. The eels were being skinned alive in full view of the customers, chopped up and thrown into a frying-pan where they continued to squirm, and on one occasion a cook pulled a live octopus out of a tank, sliced off a tentacle to add to some soup, and threw it back again. Del Giudice mentioned that the restaurant supplied short-time rooms for couples overcome by the aphrodisiac qualities of the food.

Thereafter the main object of the trip was tackled. This was a visit in the interests of folklore, Del Giudice said, to the crypt of the Cathedral in which one of the several sets of bones claimed to be those of St Andrew are kept. Three times a year, this day being one, the bones exude a miraculously rejuvenating fluid, which is collected on swabs of cotton wool and sold to the faithful. We waited for about an hour in a queue amid loud hisses of reverence and anticipation on all sides. At last Del Giudice was served, and he was lucky indeed for a few minutes later the supply ran out. The wad of cotton wool with its precious damp patch, for which he paid 200 lire, was handed to him by an attendant hunchback, which – hunchbacks being lucky – increased the efficacy of the holy substance. Del Giudice wrapped it up in a page from *Il Proletario*, and we went home.

July 12

In the months at Naples I have visited in the course of duty every town within thirty miles of the city with the exception of Pozzuoli, and a free day provided an opportunity to go there as a tourist in a CIC jeep.

There may be some hidden significance in the fact that Pozzuoli had endured the experience of our occupation with such indifference and calm. Somehow it seems to have contrived to stand apart from the war, to have been overlooked by raiding planes, and by-passed by armies whether attacking or in retreat. I found it very different both in appearance and atmosphere from any other small town in the Naples area. It was quiet and self-absorbed. There were no soldiers about, and none of the troublesome human parasites that fatten on them. It would have been quite possible to imagine that one was not in Italy at all here, but in some drowsy coastal town in the Levant. Naples is coloured in austere greys and sombre reds. Pozzuoli indulges in sedate sea-washed pinks, and hangs green shutters at its windows, many of which come to a point in the Venetian style. The presence of several cupolas heighten a Turkish effect. The people lacked the nagging curiosity of Neapolitans. Nobody found some excuse to talk to me. Nobody had anything for sale. I remembered having been told that the natives of Pozzuoli are quite separate by customs, traditions, and probably even blood from the Neapolitans, and that they speak a markedly different dialect. It may also be of

significance that Pozzuoli is outside the Zona di Camorra and
its secret tribal life, which encircles the town and reaches the
sea by way of a narrow corridor some miles to the north at
Mondragone, which is a Camorra town.

It was at Pozzuoli, and Baia – a couple of miles farther on
in the curve of the bay – that all the richest, the most profli-
gate, and the most terrible of the Romans built their seaside
villas and the gay and gracious landscape is steeped in the
black legends of their doings. Here Nero murdered his mother
Agrippina and, inviting his friends to view the body, handled
the limbs and discussed with them their good and bad points.
Here in the labyrinthine basement of the Carceri di Nerone,
he devised new tortures and experimented on his prisoners.
A mile away in his headland villa, Tiberius was smothered
by Macro, his Guards' Commander. The rings can still be
seen, seven feet under the water in the old mole of Pozzuoli,
to which the ships were fastened when Caligula brought 4000
vessels back from all parts of the Empire to construct a bridge
over the Bay, to refute a prophecy that he could no more
become Emperor than ride a horse across the Bay of Baia.

Pozzuoli put on extravagant wild-beast shows and gladia-
torial fights in its amphitheatre for the entertainment of its
holiday visitors. In AD 305 San Gennaro was thrown to the
lions there, after which, being rejected by them, he was
beheaded. A chapel has been built on the supposed site of his
martyrdom, where a piece of rock stained with his blood is
on view. The dried blood brightens in colour, and becomes
damp in sympathy and exact synchronization with the miraculous liquefaction, twice yearly, of the saint's blood in the
cathedral at Naples.

The extraordinary truncated volcano, known as the Sol-
fatara, is at the back of the town. I strolled over the surface
of its flat crater-bed, which is about three-quarters of a mile
in diameter. This, composed of a grey but glistening amalgam
of mud and crystalline sulphur, puffs vapour and bubbles
sulphurous liquid through numerous fissures. The shallow,

scrubby walls of the crater a hundred or so feet in height smoke everywhere like the sides of an old burning rubbish dump that cannot be put out. People had come here on curative pilgrimages and were standing as near as they dared to the bubbling *fumaroli* to benefit from the vapours. Others had stripped off most of their clothing and crammed themselves into artificial caves in the walls of the crater where they could cook themselves gently while drawing the sulphurous gases into their lungs.

I lunched at Vicenzo a Mare on its low cliff outside the town. They had no meat, as was to be expected in these times, but could supply *ceciniella* – tiny blind sand-eels fried in batter, followed by raw shellfish; *noci* – 'sea nuts', and *fasulari* – bean-shaped bivalves – all these specialities of the locality. They were accompanied by Falernian wine, a sparkling, sulphur-flavoured local vintage, praised by Horace, who seems to have been much impressed by everything associated with this region. While the wine might have aroused curiosity rather than admiration in a London restaurant, it was well suited for drinking on a hot day and in these surroundings. I was told that in ancient times the wine would have been served warm. It was to Vicenzo a Mare that Cuoca, last of the great Camorra chieftains, was brought, back in the 'twenties, for what was to be his funeral feast, by the underlings who had decided to depose him. Here he was feasted, praised, hugged, kissed and then – full of well-being, and at peace with the world – taken away to be stabbed to death by a specialist armed with a mattress-maker's needle.

There can be few areas of even the Mediterranean world to hold a candle to this for sheer concentration of reverberating place-names, of ruins and legend. Everywhere lie the tumbled vestiges of palaces, temples and baths. About three miles from Pozzuoli behind Monte Nuovo, a small volcano which appeared overnight on September 30, 1538, is the Lago Averno, the Lake of Avernus of the world of antiquity: a small, reed-fringed sheet of water universally believed to have been the entrance to the underworld. It was here that Aeneas was conducted by the Sibyl to the nether regions. The lake made a formidable impression on the writers and poets of those days, who were overawed by the sense of doom inspired by what they saw as its sombre surroundings, and the unearthly twilight that fell upon it with the sinking of the sun. It was believed that no bird could fly across the lake owing to its poisonous exhalations, and Homer described its shores, in the *Odyssey,* as being inhabited by the dismal and sunless Cimmerii.

Nevertheless, Lago Averno came as a disappointment. Scenically it was insignificant. I had come prepared to respect Homer's Cimmerian gloom, but the gloom was not there, neither was there any of the enchantment or the sense of mystery to be found in the lake-scenery of so many countries of the European North. The sun shone, swallows in their hundreds were dipping on the water's surface to take insects, a cheerful-looking fisherman had just come ashore and was collecting his meagre catch, and a woman hung up her washing outside a lakeside shack.

This part of Italy has few lakes to offer, and those that compete for attention with Lago Averno are the Lago de Fusaro and the Lago Lucrino, both of them quite featureless lagoons. Clearly the authors of antiquity had to do what they could with the material at hand.

Cumae is a mile away just over the hill, and here the emotional experience was of a very different order. The road passed within yards of the cliff cavern of the Sibyl, visited for counsel in their hour of extremity by so many emperors and kings of the Mediterranean world. Virgil speaks of 'its hundred entrances, and as many issues, whence sound in many voices the oracles of the prophetess'. Standing there at the mouth of this tremendous chambered corridor cut deep into the rock, it was entirely possible to believe this. Down through the openings in the cliffs, their faces pitted with innumerable caves and sanctuaries, lay the ruins of the most ancient of the

Greek colonies in Italy. Here the spell remained, and here the sense of the grandeur of the past was overwhelming. Cumae would have been worth a journey of any length.

July 24

Naples is extraordinary in every way. At the end of the last century, Scarfoglio, leading Italian journalist of his day, wrote, 'This is the only Eastern city where there is no residential European quarter,' and the witticism still seems to hold good.

Last week a nobleman in our street was lifted by his servants from his deathbed, dressed in his evening clothes, then carried to be propped up at the head of the staircase over the courtyard of his palazzo. Here with a bouquet of roses thrust into his arms he stood for a moment to take leave of his friends and neighbours gathered in the courtyard below, before being carried back to receive the last rites. Where else but in Naples could a sense of occasion be carried to such lengths?

Last week, too, Evans and I were sent to rummage through the apartment of Prince Pignatelli, whom we were told had been arrested for espionage while serving with the OSS. The apartment was like a silk-lined womb – an absurd Hollywood film-set from a De Mille Biblical epic, that wearied the eye with the glitter of gold. The Prince had gone off in a hurry to meet his fate, leaving his possessions in disarray. A satchel on a bedside table with a porphyry top contained half a million lire, and beside it stood a glass of wine into which gold leaf had been stirred. A cupboard held great flagons of Chanel perfume, and several hundred pairs of silk stockings, each pair worth the price of the honour of any woman in Naples whose honour was for sale. The impression this place gave was of the worship of luxury as a cult. A number of Neapolitan aristocrats claim descent from the great families of ancient Rome, and they may be still under the influence of legendary Roman excesses. We are told that certain Neapolitan ladies, after the custom of Poppæa Sabina, did actually take baths in milk, before the present shortages put a stop to the practice.

A few hundred yards from Pignatelli's Aladdin's cave begins the district of Vicaria where the population is the densest in Europe – possibly in the world. In Vicaria 3000 people are crammed in each acre. At this moment they live on the indescribable residue of offal bought in the slaughterhouses, on fishes' heads and tails, roots dug up in the fields, and in the last resort, it is to be supposed, even the occasional cat, since we have been told that the carcase of a rabbit is never displayed in a butcher's shop without the head that guarantees its identity.

Three hundred thousand of the population of Naples inhabit *bassi*. In the Vicaria district up to three people occupy every two square metres in a *basso*. It is to these surroundings that most street-walkers bring back their customers. The chances are, when they arrive, that there will be tenants in the room – such as bedridden old people lying in wall bunks – who have to stay. These simply turn their faces to the wall. All things in Naples are arranged with as much civility as possible.

July 26

Some of our recent adventures in the course of duty almost fall into the category of episodes from an Ashenden story by Somerset Maugham.

Last week someone had to be chosen from the Section to go to the internment camp at Padula, collect a female internee who was in some way so important that she was not even mentioned by name, and take her to Rome for interrogation. The woman was described as being of great charm and beauty, and potentially dangerous. John Dashwood, providing these intriguing details, made her sound quite like Dumas's Lady De Winter. The thing was, said John with a smirk, that she was not to be allowed out of the supervision of whoever it was took her to Rome for a single minute. While in Rome she would be deposited in the women's prison for the night, if her escort thought fit, but if he preferred not to do so he would have to devise some other means of absolutely safe custody for her.

George Hankin, the only one of us, probably, who suffers from deep religious scruples, got this job. Needless to say, the lady spent the night in prison.

My own Maugham-ish experience, two days later, was to go to Capodichino airport to collect an Italian general supposed to have been seized, drugged and kidnapped in Switzerland by members of our mysterious 100 Section, and take him to Poggio Reale. The 100 Section-man came down the steps with the General in his grip, held out his hand for my paper, subjected me to a penetrating and power-saturated look, handed over the General, shook his head at the offer of a glass of marsala, clumped back up the steps, and took off.

By contrast the General's personality seemed a cosy one. I was very sorry not to have been able to ask him the details of what had happened to him, and am quite sure that he would have been happy to unburden himself.

August 3

Salvatore Loreto, known to us for his exploits as an infiltrator and saboteur with 10th Flotilla MAS, turned up – of all places in the PW ward of Cancello Field Hospital, having been put out of action and captured on some hit-and-run mission behind our lines. I was sent to the hospital to decide whether it was secure enough to hold a man of Loreto's tigerish reputation, or whether he should be transferred to the prison infirmary in Poggio Reale. To my huge astonishment, I found in charge of the ward none other than Sister M. of the 100th General in Algeria. Here, working behind the barbed wire, and under wretched conditions of heat, flies and dust everywhere, she remained her usual charming and efficient self, and was clearly adored by the prisoners in her charge – most of whom were in dreadful shape.

Loreto was the only Italian in the ward, and he had been atrociously wounded. The Sister considered him a medical curiosity, being the only wounded man she had ever seen having a hole clean through his body, through which the light could be seen when his wounds were being dressed. When I bent over him he mistook me for his brother, put his arms round my neck, and began to weep and ramble on about episodes of our shared childhood: '*ti ricordi? . . . ti ricordi?*' – do you remember? I sat by Loreto's bed for a moment, while he went on dying from numerous causes. The Sister had done all she could for him. There were small burns on his chin from the cigarettes she had lit for him and put in his mouth, and when, after his voice had trailed off into a long silence he suddenly croaked a faint plea for one of the sweets she kept ready, she silenced him with a fruit gum.

'How long will he last?' I asked.

'Hours. Maybe a day. Two days at most. The German in the next bed is going to die soon after six o'clock.'

The head of the German in the next bed was enclosed in a kind of helmet of gauze and bandages. His face had been blown away, she said, and he had no eyes, and only a hole for a mouth. He had tried to commit suicide by tearing away the dressings from wounds in other parts of the body in the hope of provoking a fatal hæmorrhage, and now his hands were fastened by straps to the sides of his bed. He was being kept alive by nutrients and stimulants fed through a tube into a vein.

'How can you be so certain about the time?' I asked.

'I go off at six,' the Sister said. 'Tonight's my free night, and my boy-friend's coming to pick me up. While the German's alive I have to stay with him, so at six the tube will have to come out. He'd be dead by morning anyway.'

August 12

An order out of the blue to move to Benevento to take over the security from 418 Section and a detachment of Canadian FSS, all of whom are pulling out. Fortunately the arrangement by which one man will replace twenty is a temporary one, intended to last a month. I packed up my gear, left at six this morning on the motor-cycle, and was in Benevento by ten.

This ancient city of 50,000 was purposelessly destroyed in May of last year by an air-raid carried out by Flying Fortresses, and now, fifteen months later, it shows no signs of resurrection. The beautiful eleventh-century Lombard-Saracenic cathedral is only a shell, and its unique bronze doors have disappeared. I am told that only one house in five has been left standing. The custom here is to wear mourning for seven years for a close relative : father, mother, daughter or son, so the whole population is dressed in black. The poverty of these people is beyond belief. My office is in a police station, incredibly shattered by the bombing. All the ceilings are down but the plaster has just been swept into corners; sheets of cardboard are nailed over the windows. A great crack running from top to bottom of the building has been plugged with plaster-clogged wire mesh. The water supply is only turned on for a few minutes a day. One is warned to leave the tap on to collect what drips come through. Eventually a small yellow pool collects in a bowl over the dark sediment it precipitates. The porter of this place is stark naked under a torn British despatch-rider's raincoat – my first experience of an old-style *lazzarone*. On my way here I passed a row of thirteen- or fourteen-year-old *scugnizzi* sitting masturbating on the rim of a broken fountain.

The departed Canadians have left a bad memory in Benevento. It was the Sergeant-Major's habit to carry a whip with which he flogged people out of his way as he strolled through the streets. The man who controls the town now is Marshal Francesco Altamura of the SIM (Secret Police) who has been ordered by Naples to place himself at my disposal. He is handsome, good-humoured, quite imperturbable and exudes sinister power. Altamura overshadows even the 'principal citizen', who although certain to have been the local *mafioso*, appointed through Vito Genovese, is strangely ineffectual and old-maidish, and spends much of his time catering to the whims of a demanding old father.

This evening I was taken by Altamura to meet the town's notabilities. These included a prosperous coffin-maker, and the owner of what the Marshal described as the best-kept brothel in Southern Italy. The coffin-maker's business was brisk. The death-rate here would probably equal Britain's in the Middle Ages, and there was some typhus in the area. Our man's products were in exceptional demand for many miles around, being lead-lined, which, it is believed, will keep their contents intact until the Resurrection Day. I learned that the lead is from the Cathedral's roof, and had been stolen from the ruins. The brothel-keeper was first to offer a bribe. He had another establishment in Naples, closed through loss of protection by the AMG officials, who were in the pocket of his competitors. It would be worth 100,000 lire to him if someone (like me) would speak a word in the right place to get it going again.

This overture reminded me of a slip of paper handed over by the member of 418 Section from whom I took over. I read it again:

CARABINIERE	100 Lire
BRIGADIERE	200 Lire
MARESCIALLO	Mozzarella cheese
PRINCIPAL CITIZEN	Spaghetti (Tagliatelle preferred), or Mozzarella cheese
COMMISSARIO PS	Bottle Sarti
MARCHESA M.	Keating's Powder or similar

These were the small customary gifts which changed hands in

exchange for any small service that might be performed.

The question of a car came up, this being essential to my work. Only five were registered in the town, but the Marshal believed he could find one. We went to a garage and I was shown a Bianchi standing on wood blocks in a corner. Besides the wheels, a number of engine parts were missing. No one so far, said the Marshal, had been able to requisition this car, but many had tried. He believed that all the missing parts could be found, and it could be made available to a friend. What he was in effect saying was, with me you swim – without me you sink. While these matters were being discussed I strolled round and picked up a tyre on a bench. This was a Dunlop cover from the walls of which the trade-name, number and size had been removed, and nearby was an electrical tool with which this operation had clearly been performed. Another tyre possessed a Dunlop tread, but with Pirelli lettering on the wall. I asked the garage man where these stolen tyres came from, and he told me he bought them. 'Everybody does.' He was a friend of the Marshal's, and ready to be a friend of mine. And he, and everyone else, knows I depend on the Marshal.

It was dark by the time we returned to the office. On our way back I noticed zigzagging points of light and occasionally small showers of sparks in the sky and pointed these out to the Marshal. He explained that the boys caught bats, tied rags soaked in petrol to them, set light to the rags and then let them go. He was full of praise for the ingenuity with which they made their own small pleasures, but acknowledged with regret that the petrol had probably been stolen out of someone's tank.

August 13

Today a begrimed and bedraggled waif calling herself Giuseppina appeared at the office. This alert 12-year-old would tell me nothing about herself other than her age, that her parents had been killed in the great bombing, and that she lived 'under a house' down by the river. There are boy-orphans by the hundred like her, barefooted, ragged and hungry, but somehow managing to survive and fill the gaunt streets with their laughter, but this was the first abandoned girl I had seen. Giuseppina told me she had come for her blanket as usual.

I was astonished. Blankets are one form of currency in this Italy in ruins – but currency of a fairly high denomination, good Australian or Canadian specimens fetching the equivalent of a low-grade factory-worker's weekly wage. I told her I had no blankets to give away, and offered her a packet of army biscuits, which she gracefully refused. 'Isn't this still the police station?' she asked. I agreed that it was, and she told me that the man who had been here before – clearly my Canadian predecessor – had given her a blanket once a week.

Only at this point did I realize the tragic significance of the request, and that this skinny, undeveloped little girl was a child prostitute. The *scugnizzi* of Naples and Benevento are intelligent, charming and above all philosophical – notably more so than children from protected homes – and this female version of the breed was in no way different from her male counterparts. Much as she may have been disappointed by my rejection of her services, nothing but good humour showed in her face. She bobbed something like a curtsy. 'Perhaps I'll take the biscuits after all,' she said. Then, with a wave, she was off.

August 15

The Marchesa mentioned on my friend's list turned out to be the last surviving member of one of the great hereditary landowning families in the neighbourhood. She appeared to be between fifty and sixty years of age, was laden with jewellery, yellowed with fever, and smoked a pipe. She had the reputation for nymphomania, and in the files left by my predecessor it was alleged that it was her habit to bribe teenage *scugnizzi* to accompany her on horseback rides to a wood some miles out of town, where they were seduced and rewarded with payments of 50 lire.

I was received in the small habitable portion of her castle. There were pigeons in the rafters over our head, and the floor was thick with their droppings. She lived by supplying pigeons to the local hotel, and let out the keep and the bell-tower to pig-breeders. The floor of the banqueting hall had been covered with soil, and in this she grew vegetables. She was clearly a woman of great energy.

The Marchesa claimed to be of Swabian ancestry and told me that only French was allowed to be spoken in the castle when she was a child. Her contempt for the Italian peasantry was measureless, and she boasted of the feudal oppressions committed by her family, claiming that their vassals were even taxed (twenty-one nights a month) for sleeping with their wives. She knows everyone in the province and it is valuable to have a point of view differing dramatically from that of the Marshal. One astonishing allegation : that the harmless and effete-looking principal citizen controlled a powerful band of outlaws. These had got their hands on a damaged tank which they were rebuilding. She warned me that I would soon be approached with a request for spare parts 'for a tractor'.

August 18

I have temporarily moved into the Hotel Vesuvio, once pride of the town, and possessing not only ten bedrooms but the only Turkish bath in the province. The hotel has been concentrated and simplified following damage suffered in the great air-raid. Now only one large room remains, a corner of which contains some twenty or thirty hatstands, as many spittoons, and a small grove of potted palms. This room, according to the hour of day, serves as café or restaurant, and punctually at midnight Japanese screens are produced, and four iron beds normally standing on end against the walls are lifted into position. I sleep on one of these, much troubled by the mosquitoes and the heat.

A problem has arisen. Although I handed in my army rations to the cook, with the intention of living on these, nobody has taken me seriously, nor believed that any human being in his right mind and able to eat pasta would refrain from doing so. Consequently at every meal a plateful of spaghetti is placed in front of me. Alberto the proprietor is a kind and generous man, and it seems hard to push this aside untouched without causing hurt feelings. The difficulty is to find some way of reciprocating this hospitality, bearing in mind the Italian belief that any Allied soldier has access to unlimited supplies of food. Yesterday, while drawing rations as arranged from the South Africans at San Giorgio, it occurred to me to ask the sergeant if there happened to be any tins of meat going begging. He readily produced a half-dozen large cans of bacon, described as terrible stuff which nobody would eat. These I took back to the hotel and handed over to Alberto, suggesting that he should invite all his friends round for supper.

The party proved a huge success. In addition to the social elite of Benevento I already knew : Marshal Altamura, the principal citizen, the Marchesa and the coffin-maker, Don Enrico – the local capitalist – who is Alberto's sleeping partner in the business, came along. He had the sad eyes and the drooping features of a bloodhound, and the nails of his little fingers had been allowed to grow enormously long to prove – in the old-fashioned style of the South – that he did no work. Three tables were shoved together, and the potted palms arranged to screen us from the regular guests. We were served by Lina, the maid-of-all-work, scrubbed up, starched and gloved for the occasion, and quite unrecognizable as the slattern who came creeping in behind the Japanese screens most nights to bring solace to some commercial traveller for the reasonable fee of 50 lire. Her mother, a crone in black, kept the wonderful old horned gramophone going with scratched Verdi records. After some experiment it had been decided to eat the bacon raw. No one present had ever tasted bacon before, and all were ecstatic in their praise. Tumblerfuls of the sour but powerful local wine went to most heads. The Marchesa bellowed her laughter across the room, scattered ash everywhere from her pipe, and was taken with a paroxysm of coughing when Alberto went dashing round to spray the palms with Flit. Don Enrico, a copy of whose grovelling letter, written to Hitler in person, had found its way into my hands, held an American flag upside down, and kept up a monotonous cracked-voice chanting *Vivono gli Alleati*. At a late stage a drunken attempt to sing the National Anthem broke down into the Triumphal March from *Aïda*. When it was all over I felt that at least I had broached local reserve, and done something towards putting to rest the spectre of the whip-cracking sergeant-major.

Tonight the Bianchi was delivered to the hotel, for my use while in Benevento – on loan.

August 20

The Marshal is, or appears to be, worried. He says the town is surrounded by bandits, and he has heard that they may link up and attack it. What did I propose to do?

Nothing, I said. It's none of my business.

'We're all in this together,' he said. 'You could catch it in the neck, too.'

I asked him what he proposed, and his suggestion was that we ought to go out for the baddies before they came after us.

With what? I asked him. What could we produce in the way of men and weapons? I mentioned that I had a ·38 Webley with five rounds only of ammunition – the same gun and the same ammunition with which I landed at Salerno a year ago. The Marshal, who packs a Beretta automatic, could call on the support of three Carabinieri, but as they only had two pairs of military boots between them, only two men were available at a time for any active duty. They were armed with

Carcano rifles dating from about 1912 – the weapon which helped the Italians to lose this war. There were two Pubblica Sicurezza men who, he says, would run away as soon as the first shot was fired. Finally a detachment of two British Military Police was stationed in the town, and might agree to give a hand.

I objected that the bandits, who in the main were Italians and American army deserters, were known to be armed with Breda heavy machine-guns. Not only that, he agreed, but all the latest American equipment. He understood that this had been secretly supplied by OSS agents. He claimed to know that the ultimate intention was to form these irregulars into a Separatist army in support of the secret movement to detach the whole of the South of Italy from the North. From this it seemed that Lattarullo's Separatist friends, improbable collection as they might be, could be gaining ground here, as we know that they are in Sicily.

'We have to do something,' he says. 'The longer we leave it the worse it'll get.' I then remembered that a signal had just come in to say that reinforcements were on their way, composed of two Canadian half-sections, totalling two officers, two sergeant-majors, and eight sergeants. I decided to keep this piece of information to myself.

At this point I brought up the fact that today the principal citizen asked me to get him parts for his tractor. 'Are these actually for a tank?' I asked.

The Marshal shrugged his shoulders. 'You shouldn't believe all you hear,' he said. 'I suppose they could be.'

August 21

Discussed the problem of the bandits with Don Ubaldo, the schoolmaster, who said they have always been there in times of trouble. He remembered them in his childhood before and after the 1914 war, and could recall no period of history when Southern Italy and Sicily had been free from this nuisance for any length of time. I told him that although little mention is made of them in the newspapers I have learned through our section in Sicily that up to thirty bands were in operation there at this time, many of them believed to be led by common criminals who had succeeded in escaping from gaol during the fighting.

Don Ubaldo said that by tradition, when law and order had collapsed, many of these attached themselves to the great land-owners, who gave them shelter and a little food in exchange for their services in keeping the peasantry in order. At this moment in Sicily they were raiding police stations and Allied dumps for arms, and occasionally they attacked isolated villages. Don Ubaldo had never heard of an attack on a town the size of Benevento; however – as there were no Allied troops in the vicinity – he was afraid they might be tempted. This schoolmaster, who is officially inscribed in one of the innumerable left-wing political parties, said that most people were now beginning to see the era of Fascism as a golden interlude of security and firm government.

He related an anecdote of the extermination of the last of the nineteenth-century brigands in a small town nearby. They were surrounded in a house, and the police couldn't get them out. Every time they tried to break in someone was shot. In the end the priest was called in to act as a go-between. He got the police to agree that if the brigands surrendered, there would be no more bloodshed. The brigands gave in, and it was decided to kill them all the same, but as the police captain was not prepared to break his word about shedding blood, they were smothered one by one in a bed.

August 25

Peters, the MP sergeant, had a lucky escape in an encounter with the bandits on the Nola road only a mile out of town. They tossed a grenade into his jeep, but this fortunately fell in the space behind the back seat, and the seat's metal back

protected him from the blast and the fragments. He came
out of it with only a damaged ear-drum.

Conference to decide what is to be done. The Town Major,
a pure cypher, suggested appeal to the nearest infantry unit
for loan of a company. The first objection was we'd never get
one, and the second, that they'd be useless in this situation if
we did. The bandits have their own intelligence system and
as soon as any body of soldiers moved in their direction they'd
simply pull back into the hills. Peters turned out to be a
marvellous old regimental sweat with a Palestinian campaign-
ribbon, white-Blancoed to the eyes, and as expressionless as a
trained butler. Said that the bandits, who were now fully
motorized, were driving an ex-German army lorry.

Decision : to wait for the arrival of the FS sections, and then
perhaps take action.

August 28

The news is that Benevento is now officially suffering from
two epidemics : smallpox and typhoid. Ninety cases of typhoid
have been reported, but there are no figures for smallpox. Nor
are there any figures for the cases of typhus – from which there
have been a number of deaths – including that of the Carabinieri captain who was the Marshal's predecessor. In speaking
of this some days ago, the Marshal mentioned with perhaps a
touch of relish that this officer was from Rome. 'These Roman
gentlemen don't seem to take root down here,' he said. 'They
arrive so full of energy and enthusiasm, but they can't get
used to the conditions. They take pills all the time and cover
themselves with all sorts of powder, but they go out like
candles.' Having said this, I felt his speculative gaze fall on me.
'To be able to put up with a place like this,' the Marshal said,
'your blood has to be like mine – too strong for the mosquitoes,
fleas and lice.'

For myself the chief worry was the possibility of another
bout of malaria. I took double doses of mepacrine – which

was slowly turning my skin and the whites of my eyes yellow – slept under a mosquito net, and rubbed stinking mosquito repellent into all the exposed parts of my skin, but I got bitten all the same. People accept malaria as a matter of course in this town.

Here, to all intents and purposes, we were living in the Middle Ages. Only the buildings had changed – and most of these were in ruins. Epidemics, robbers, funerals followed by shrieking women, deformed and mutilated beggars, legless cripples dragging themselves about on wheeled platforms – even raving lunatics they'd no room for in the asylum. People walked the streets with handkerchiefs pressed over their mouths and noses as they probably did in the days of the plagues of old. This morning I actually found myself in a little square tucked away among the ruins where women were dancing to drive the sickness away.

August 30

Went to the Hotel Vesuvio for lunch where one of Don Ubaldo's friends arrived with the news that he has been taken ill. He had a prescription for medicine urgently required, but – although one can buy every kind of fancy cake or sweet in Benevento – there is no medicine. Could I help in any way?

I was due to go into Naples with my weekly report, so I left immediately in the Bianchi, covering the distance, including all the detours where the bridges were down, in a couple of hours, and took the prescription to my contact in the pharmaceutical world. There was no problem. My friend had every drug known to modern medicine, and I knew where his abundant supplies had come from. While waiting for the prescription to be made up I wandered round the counter to inspect the activities of a small boy who was busily soaking off English labels before sticking on Italian ones. It was no business of mine to interfere, and it would have made no difference had I done so. All I should have done was lose a friend, and Don Ubaldo's medicine into the bargain. I am gradually becoming drawn into the system!

August 31

Back to Benevento where I delivered the medicine for Don Ubaldo, who now appeared to be gravely ill, though I was not told with what. Saw a funeral with a professional mourner who tore at her cheeks with her fingernails, and drew blood. Also an Italian sanitary team chasing peasants to spray them with anti-typhus powder. The peasants did not know what was happening to them, and some were hooting with fear.

This afternoon the promised Canadians arrived in two splendid Dodge lorries, and proved to be the wildest of real-life gun-slinging cowboys, straight from the prairies. They have everything that any soldier can possibly want: an assortment of guns, hip-flasks, poker-dice, signed photos of Rita Hayworth, pocketfuls of french letters and occupation money. One sergeant has a diamond as big as my thumbnail taken in exchange for the bundles of thousand-lire notes acquired somewhere along the line. The diamond, he explained, is wealth in its most portable form. There are twelve Canadians: two captains, two sergeant-majors and eight sergeants, and the atmosphere is democratic. Nobody salutes anybody and the captains are called by their first names. On hearing of the possibility of a clash with bandits there were whoops of enthusiasm. The enthusiasm flagged this evening over the pre-dinner drinks when one of them spotted a guest of the Vesuvio sitting quietly in his corner being sick into a bag and was told that the man might be in the first stages of a highly infectious and usually fatal sickness. They have a wholly American and New World terror of poor hygiene, and are appalled by the dirtiness of Italy, a prejudice which did not prevent two of them from making their arrangements for tonight with the maid-of-all-work, whose general appearance is unhealthy to say the least.

September 1

A single night in the stifling communal dormitory of the Hotel
Vesuvio, under the attack of its very special breed of house
mosquito, has been enough to break some Canadian spirits,
and this morning the two officers, a sergeant-major and four
sergeants decided to move on to Avellino where conditions
were reported better. I was therefore left with the other
sergeant-major and four sergeants. They are friendly and co-
operative – and in spite of their amorality, hard to dislike.
They have absolutely nothing whatever to do with their time,
and hardly know what the war is about. As was to be expected,
not one of them speaks a word of Italian. Today has been spent
in getting to know the town. They give candy to every child
in sight, shove all male Italians off the pavement, and make
an instant sexual advance to every woman of child-bearing
age they encounter. These routine approaches are endured by
the girls with great dignity, and some go to the lengths of
making polite and even apologetic speeches explaining just
why they feel unable to agree to have sexual intercourse on
the spot.

The Canadians object very much to flies, which I have
learned to live with, as there is nothing that can be done about
them. These flies of Benevento are constantly in search of
moisture, and when one lands on a Canadian lip or eyelid
and begins to suck, it usually provokes a whinny of disgust.
This afternoon we saw a man lying in the street, probably at
death's door, being carefully avoided by passers-by, all with
their handkerchiefs pressed over their noses. Jason, the
youngest, wildest and most likeable of the Canadians, suggested
ringing up the hospital and having an ambulance sent, and
was surprised to be told that the phones do not work, the
hospital has no ambulance, that one nurse who goes home at
night looks after a hundred patients, and that there is not
room to cram one single patient more into the floor space

between the beds.

Gloom deepened at the Vesuvio tonight at the news that Don Ubaldo is not expected to live, and that people are beginning to leave the town in panic.

The services of the maid-of-all-work having been reserved in advance for tonight by one of her regulars, I suggested to two of the Canadians in a romantic frame of mind that they might care to see what the local brothel had to offer. They went off, but were soon back complaining that the only girl available had a glass eye.

September 3

Don Ubaldo died of typhoid this morning.

In response to urgent requests from the Canadians that we move out of town I saw the principal citizen, who was clearly delighted to perform a service he might be able to cash in on at some later date, and also, no doubt, to see the back of us. He immediately found an empty farmhouse in the village of Sagranella, up in the hills, and within a couple of hours of seeing him we had installed ourselves there. The farmhouse is vast, clean and archaic – giving the sensation of living in a cave above ground, and it has magnificent views over the bare hills which, when we arrived, glittered like copper under the midday sun. This village seems hardly to have moved out of the Bronze Age. I am told it has a fox-cult, and every year a fox is captured and burned to death, and its tail is hung, like a banner, from a pole at the village's entrance. There is an enormous Easter Island-style head in a field nearby, which spares a sardonic smile for the passer-by, and which probably dates from Samnite times – or before. It is said that the *droit du seigneur* is practised as a matter of course on the neighbouring big estate, which seems to be cultivated almost entirely by women. They leave the village to go to work just before dawn, and return shortly after dark – a 16-hour day. The steward is said to feel a woman's muscles before employing her.

The great and extraordinary attraction of this place is the presence of myriads of fireflies in the bushy slopes beneath us, and tonight, with the darkness, every bush carried its own soft, bluish illumination, and every leaf and branch was separately and glowingly lit up. This delighted the Canadians, who show a childlike wonderment for such new experiences. One of the few buildings of note spared by the American bombing was the Strega factory, where one can buy a bottle of amber-coloured, aromatic liqueur for the reasonable sum of 100 lire, plus one pound of sugar. It turned out that the Canadians carried even a supply of sugar in their Dodge, so earlier in the day we had gone over to the factory and bought a dozen bottles. With these a house-warming took place at the farmhouse tonight, and the Canadians, instantly drunk on the strong, sticky liquor, stripped off their clothes and went dancing and singing out of the house and down the hillside among the bushes and the fireflies – an unearthly and even poetic sight.

September 6

The Canadians are generous and open-handed in every way. Bred in the freedom of limitless spaces, property, possessions and territorial rights of any kind seem to mean less to them than those things do to us. Anything they have is yours for the asking : their transport, their booze, or even a personally autographed picture of Rita. Unhesitatingly, and as a matter of course, a share is offered in the two dazed peasant girls picked up on one of their forays, whom they treat like pet monkeys, and feed with biscuits and scraps of bacon at odd times all through the day. They have run out of whisky, and I have some misgivings about the sweet and ensnaring Strega. This they drink by the tumblerful, even for breakfast, after which, buckling on their guns, they go staggering off in search of adventure.

*

To my surprise, definite occupation was found for me on my last visit to HQ: to investigate the motives of a clandestine political party operating in this area. Some sixty-five political parties have now been inscribed with our blessing and will take part in the wild democratic free-for-all to be expected when elections are held. In addition there are many un-recognized movements aspiring to lead the nation back to greatness. Most of these are freakish, like Lattarullo's Separatists who want to dress people in Roman tunics, enforce a legal minimum of ten children per family, and reintroduce serfdom in one guise or another. Some are regarded as more purposeful and sinister including the one to be investigated, called Forza Italia!, which is suspected of Neo-Fascist leanings. My contacts in Benevento dismiss it with scorn as just another maniac right-wing movement backed by the landlords and the rural Mafia, run in this case by a half-demented *latifundista* who proclaims himself a reincarnation of Garibaldi. However, a report has been ordered, so, learning that a public meeting was to be held today in San Marco di Cavali, a hill village in the Monti del Sannio about 30 miles away, I asked the Canadians for the loan of their Dodge, and went up there, leaving at about six before any of my friends were astir, and arrived at about eight.

Political meetings in the far South are held early to avoid the worst heat, and they often provide the excuse for the organization of an impromptu fair. In this case people who had come to hear the speeches had also taken the opportunity to bring a few sheep with them for sale, and a stall selling toys made out of plaited straw, maize-flour cakes, and tin pan-pipes, had been set up, and a three-man band waited to play. San Marco seemed to have been carved out of the bone of the mountain, a human coral, where the fight against misery left nothing much over for anybody in the way of a life. It was a village of shepherds with totem-pole faces, solemn and silent men born into a life hardly distinguishable from slavery. In some cases it may have been real slavery, because it was commonly said that in this and many other districts in the South young boys were secretly sold by their parents to the owners of large flocks. These taciturn men were bigger and tougher-looking than Southern Italian peasants, with whom I suspect they have little in common.

All the political speeches of these days seem to be interchangeable, platitudinous stuff. Italian audiences enjoy oratory unrelated to argument, and are attracted to a display of verbal fireworks normally used to conceal absence of original thought. Although the speaker in this case was nominally a subversive, he had nothing whatever new to say, and certainly nothing likely in any way to endanger the security of the Allied forces. He ranted and raved on interminably, and a few of the shepherd audience broke their habit of silence to grunt their approval. I stood there for a while, and took a few notes to base a report on. My feeling was one of extreme isolation. I was also highly conspicuous – and therefore the object of some curiosity – in a village where it was possible that no British soldier had set foot before.

After about an hour I felt that I knew all I wanted to know about the Forza Italia! movement, and going back to where I had left the Dodge in a patch of shade, I was surprised to find it surrounded by about fifty men, who turned to face me as I walked towards them. Their appearance was hostile. Two men had been looking into the back of the lorry over the tailboard, and going to see what it was all about, I found perhaps half the floor covered with sticky, not quite dried-out blood, which I realized must have been there when I left Sagranella. The implacable neolithic faces were closing in, and I had the feeling that at any moment I might be rushed. I forced my way through the crowd, climbed into the cabin and started up. Edging forward through the rampart of bodies, as the shouts started and fists were raised, the possibility occurred to me that these shepherds had had some encounter with one of the killer squads of the German army, had watched me taking notes, and assumed me to be the equivalent of a Gestapo executioner. Then, seeing the blood in the lorry, they had concluded it had been used to remove the victims of summary killings. I left San Marco followed by howls of execration and a few flying stones.

Back in Sagranella among the continued feasting and revelry in the farmhouse, the mystery was explained almost cheerfully. Late last night the Canadians had run a civilian down, more or less amputating his legs, and had put him in the back of the Dodge, driven him to Campobasso Hospital, and there left him. No one could possibly have been more sincerely apologetic when they heard about my embarrassment in San Marco.

September 11

While the war's emergencies continue to absorb the attention, Benevento seems no different from any other ruined town, but in the moments of calm and reflection its atmosphere asserts itself, and one catches a whiff of fear.

A *scugnizzio* appeared at the office at about eleven o'clock to say that a man he didn't know had sent him to tell me that someone had just been shot dead by a *lupara* – the sawn-off shotgun used in ritual killings – and left lying in the street outside the Café Roma. I went there as soon as I could but found nothing – only little rivulets of blood on the cobbles where a body might have lain. People hurried past, heads turned in the other direction. A waiter was clearing a table in the café, and I went and asked him if he had seen or heard anything unusual. He shook his head. The one behind the bar hadn't either. My friend Alberto in the Vesuvio, a hundred yards away from the Café Roma, had had a completely uneventful morning. So had Don Enrico, the capitalist, who had been drinking coffee substitute in the Vesuvio at about that time. Lina, the maid-of-all-work, thought she might have heard a car backfire but couldn't be sure. All these people had been bred to silence. They were drugged with caution. They had trained themselves to deal with all such questions with a bland smile, to hear or see nothing. The Marshal said, 'Someone's been pulling your leg. If anything had happened I'd be the first to know.'

Being still unsatisfied I went back to the *scugnizzi*, who don't seem to be afraid of anything, and remain the major source of unsullied truth. I questioned a couple of them and both agreed that there had been a murder and a number of people had seen it. I, too, was sure now that there had. Why should people want to pull the wool over my eyes? A rather spine-chilling start to the day.

September 16

The news is that Bernard Durham of our section has been wounded in a drive against bandits in Avellino. His attacker, dressed as an American officer, leaped from a car held up at a check-point and drilled him through the shoulder at close-range with a ·45 automatic. This is the Section's first casualty. Fortunately Durham was not seriously injured. This could well be the same gang who have been troubling us in Benevento, because Peters, the MP sergeant, reported the presence of an American in the lorry on the occasion when the hand-grenade was thrown into his jeep.

The question is how to deal with this business of the bandits, because the problem instantly arises as to what extent I am personally involved – or should be involved. However vague my function may be in practice, basically I am in Benevento in the interests of the security of British troops. Bandits – so long as the bandits are not bothering us – seem to me a problem for the Italian police. The Canadians don't agree, and I am supposed to advise them but not give them orders. They are longing for a scrap with anyone, and are a law unto themselves. Sergeant Peters, still angry over the grenade attack, says his orders cover any action he decides to take, and he sides with the Canadians. Marshal Altamura, eyes a-glitter with schemes, pleads for assistance in maintaining law and order. The more I see of him the more unhappy I feel about my enforced alliance with this man. One of my daily crop of anonymous letters has accused him of involvement with one of the bands. Should there be any truth in this, it is on the cards that he is out to arrange for the elimination of a rival organization – possibly the one said to be controlled by the principal citizen. A labyrinth of intrigue.

A meeting was held today to decide what is to be done. The Marshal said he had received information that bandits will come into the town tomorrow night by the direct road from Foggia, with the intention of picking up arms and equipment. He argued that Field Security must be involved because enemy agents and saboteurs used the travel facilities offered by the bandits to move about the country. It was agreed to set up a check-point on the Foggia road, and it was also agreed that FS would limit its interest to problems arising out of unauthorized travel. Any other action would be the responsibility of the Italian police.

September 19

Spent most of the day reconnoitring the outskirts of Benevento and the roads leading into and out of the town, as well as collecting wildly conflicting advice from contacts as to the possible movements of the bandits. It was decided to set up the check-point about three miles out of town just across the Ufita river, where the bridge was down. This lonely second-class road was the natural choice of all clandestine traffic from the South, and from the Adriatic coast.

By about ten o'clock we were in position. A brilliant night, with every house and tree clear-cut under a warm, reddish moon. High summer, burning away all traces of green vegetation by day, had brought out small fragrant night flowers all round us, and fireflies were winking everywhere in the scrub.

The Canadians, laden with weaponry and Strega, were jubilantly excited, the Carabinieri nervously resigned, the British MPs inscrutably correct. A heterogeneous force, but alas with no one in control.

There was no shortage of clandestine travellers. A Carabiniere with a lamp waved the cars and lorries into the roadside, and the passengers tumbled out of them, their faces whitened like clowns by the dust. About one in ten was authorized to be making the journey. Those who were not produced a miscellany of scraps of paper wheedled out of Allied officers who were not entitled to issue passes, or passes that were out of date, or not valid for this particular journey, or that were straightforward forgeries. Every vehicle was stocked with contraband of one kind or another, and this was joyfully off-loaded by the Marshal, in theory to be taken according to the regulations to the municipal depot. Since a drum of olive oil was worth about 50,000 lire on the black market, one wondered how much of this treasure would really finds its way to the *ammasso*. There were pleadings, offers of bribes, tears – and almost certainly whispered deals. I was alarmed at one moment to realize that the Marshal was no longer with us, then to see him come into view from behind some bushes with a young lady who then quietly and complacently took her seat again in the lorry she'd been travelling in.

The Canadians had discovered that most cars were travelling on stolen tyres. These they ordered to be removed on the spot, although I feared less out of zeal for the protection of Allied property than from the knowledge that every serviceable tyre would fetch 30,000 lire, and no questions asked.

By great good luck the routine travellers had been dealt with and cleared off the scene before the bandits arrived. It could have been two or three in the morning in the flat, dead moonlight when we were beginning to yawn at each other, and in my case hallucination had crept into the fatigue brought on by three sleepless nights. The familiar cocoon of dust of an approaching lorry failed this time to alert us. The lorry, going fast, slowed as it approached the barrier, switched off its lights, then accelerated again to sweep the Carabiniere with the lamp aside, and go crashing through. It passed us in a sprinkling of shots, and a disorderly rush to take up firing positions. Reaching the end of the demolished bridge, it swung aside, lowered itself carefully down the river bank, trundled through the stones and the thin current of the river bed, and began to climb the opposite bank, already safe from the fusillades of the Carabinieri's toy weapons, and out of accurate range of the Thompson sub-machine-gun fired by Peters, the MP sergeant.

The emergency had caught the Canadians' Dodge facing in the wrong direction, and for some reason the Bren, mounted on its tripod, couldn't be swivelled through 180 degrees. The bandits' lorry was on the skyline on the farther bank for only a matter of seconds before the Dodge could be started and manœuvred into a position where the Bren could be used. Jason at the Bren fired an excited half-clip. We saw the sparkle of the bullets' impact on metal, then the lorry dropped down below the skyline, and the Dodge went off in chase. Our attention was now wrenched away by the sudden apparition and stoppage 200 yards short of the ruined barricade of a second lorry. We saw a number of figures leave it and make for the shelter of an olive grove, and we began to run towards them. I found myself with one of the Carabinieri recruits and tried to keep close to him. Someone had thrust a Thompson into my hands which I knew only vaguely how to operate, and I was filled with a drowsy determination to avoid killing or getting killed. We ran forward in a slow, lumbering fashion into the empty lanes of olives, which repeated themselves like a wallpaper pattern. Roots tripped us up, we slumped into dry irrigation ditches, and the nightjars flapped away from us like enormous moths. Then a tall, thin Negro capered into sight ahead, facing us. I saw a sad, elongated head thrusting from the jacket of an American uniform, a Schmeisser sub-machine-gun held in the crook of the right arm, and the left arm dangling as if damaged. Shots were crackling a long way away. The Negro, his mouth hanging open, and capering and ducking like a boxer, swung his gun from one to the other of us, as if to wave us away. I pointed the Thompson in the direction of his thighs, pressed the trigger, and a single *clunk* announced that it had jammed. The young Carabiniere dropped to one knee to aim his popgun Carcano. He fired and the Negro flopped over backwards weightlessly, like a hollow figure in a fairground shooting range, and then, to my relief, scrabbling about with arms and legs, began to get up again. We came in on both sides of him. There was a black stripe across the top of his forehead going back through his hair, where the bullet had miraculously grazed his skull without penetrating it. He wobbled about showing the white palms of his hands, and then the young Carabiniere jumped on him, pulled him down, and handcuffed him. The Carabiniere pulled out a length of lightweight chain. He attached this to the handcuffs, pulled the Negro to his feet, then led him away to be chained to a treestump, just as if he were chaining up a bicycle. The Negro sat down among the fireflies and put his head in his hands, and a little blood began to ooze through his fingers. Not a word had passed between the three of us.

We heard the Bren distantly, beating a slow, deliberate tattoo, then silence. Another Carabiniere and a Pubblica Sicurezza agent dressed for the city streets in a double-breasted suit materialized quietly from leaves and moonlight to tell us that escaping bandits were hiding in the farmhouses. The walls of one of these gleamed like a paper cut-out at the end of the grove. We left the chained-up Negro and ran to it, and an old bearded man, startled and innocent in his long nightshirt, let us in. It was a human byre with beds everywhere, full of the sharp smell of the goats nestling in their urine-soaked straw behind low partition walls. The PS agent scampered about pulling down bed-covers and shining his torch into the faces of men and women who pretended to be asleep, and chickens, disturbed in the rafters above us, flapped about to keep their balance.

'Who's this fellow?' the agent asked.

'My nephew, you mean?' the old man asked.

The agent caught him by the throat and smacked his face several times, without much indignation or force.

'You mother's arse-hole! No, I don't mean your nephew. Why's he got all his clothes on? Why's he bleeding?'

'Bleeding is he, eh?'

'Yes, he's bleeding. Madonna, there's blood everywhere. God in a shit-house, there's blood all over the floor!'

The agent shone his torch down at our feet, then bent down to dip the tip of his finger in a small black puddle. 'This,' he said, 'is blood.'

The old man straightened himself and spoke with dignity. 'A man comes to my house at night, tells me he's tired and wants a bed. I don't ask questions. We're Christians.'

The man in the bed, understanding now that the game was up, began to writhe and moan. A further examination showed that he had been hit twice in the thigh. The agent handcuffed him to the bed, told the old man to put his clothes on and come with us, and we went off to find the rest.

At the check-point we found the Canadians, the MPs and the Marshal reassembled. The Canadians had shot the bandits' lorry to pieces, but most of the bandits had managed to get away. For all that, we had eight prisoners – two of them wounded, including our Negro (inevitably an American deserter) – with no casualties on our side. One of the prisoners, a handsome youth of about eighteen, brought in grinning with fear, had a huge sum of money on him, and Jason made the unbelievable suggestion that he be allowed to take this boy out of sight, shoot him, and keep the money. I could not at the time make up my mind whether this was a silly joke, or whether the suggestion – put in a half-jesting manner – was to test my reaction. For all his wildness, Jason had always seemed to me good-hearted, but now he alarmed me. I was beginning also to see that the situation in Benevento was one from which I should do what I could to extricate myself as soon as possible.

September 20

A bad start to the week. A visit to the *ammasso* failed to uncover evidence that anything but trivial amounts of olive oil had been deposited there after last night's seizures. The *Responsabile* was in turn shifty, evasive and sullen, and later, when tackled on the subject, the Marshal was equally unforthcoming. Asked what had become of the confiscated tyres, he said he hadn't the faintest idea, and could only presume that the Canadians had taken charge of them. This the Canadians denied. The Marshal wanted to make me a present of a showy watch, and was offended when I turned the offer down. These days his habitual geniality seemed to be wearing thin.

I am beginning to feel that the cooling in the Marshal's attitude reflects a change in feeling of the townspeople in general. The friends I have made have suddenly become overpolite, in this way debarring me from access even to that tiny portion of their private thoughts to which I was once admitted. Open criticism would be unthinkable but I have already heard in a most roundabout way that the arrest of the farmer De Micco for sheltering the wounded bandit has met with general disapproval. 'Who wouldn't have done the same thing?' I suspect that people see us – the Canadians, the MPs and myself – as being manipulated by the Marshal, and they secretly despise us for our weakness and our blindness in allowing this to happen.

The fact is that we have upset the balance of nature here. I personally have been rigid when I should have been flexible. Here the police – corrupt and tyrannical as they are – and the civil population play a game together, but the rules are complex and I do not understand them, and through lack of this understanding, I lose respect. Every single person who comes to the office to ask me for a travel pass puts a 100-lire note down on the desk, and I push it away. What I cannot and must not in my position accept, is the fact that these people are not offering what we think of as a bribe, but making a routine gesture of courtesy. This is an African tribal system in which every well-bred person expects to give and receive dashes. My predecessor, who was more flexible than I, handed out dashes in accordance with the list he left me. This I have not done, and by failing to do so I am probably dismissed as ill-mannered and avaricious. By this failure to exchange ritual gifts I have almost certainly lost friends.

I'm probably making too much fuss about the missing tyres and olive oil, and suspect that this isn't really the way these things should be done. It may well be that to keep my position and respect, what I should do is turn my back on the whole episode, acknowledge gracefully that I've lost a trick, and avoid making difficulties for those – and there may be many of them – who have benefited from the windfall.

September 23

I have left the Canadians in their stronghold in Sagranella and moved back into the Hotel Vesuvio, where this evening I received a distressing confirmation of my fear that I may now be considered a potential or actual *jettatore*, a possessor of the evil eye. When I first moved into the hotel I noticed that Don Enrico, enthroned in his wicker armchair in a position in which he could keep under observation every person who entered or left the hotel, occasionally groped in his pocket to touch his testicles on the appearance of a stranger. This, Don Ubaldo explained to me, was a precaution – commonplace in the South, but frequently practised by Northerners, including Mussolini himself – to ward off the evil eye. On two or three occasions in the last week I have noticed women hastily cover their faces with a scarf or a veil at my approach, and scuttle past with averted faces. This, apparently, is how women deal with the problem. Now, this evening, coming into the hotel,

I found a row of half a dozen regulars – Don Enrico included – sitting under the palms, and at the sight of me I seemed to notice a sly movement of every left hand towards the right side of the crutch. A disconcerting confirmation of loss of favour.

In any case, setting aside all questions of my personal shortcomings, I have arrived at a time when, in their hearts, these people must be thoroughly sick and tired of us. A year ago we liberated them from the Fascist Monster, and they still sit doing their best to smile politely at us, as hungry as ever, more disease-ridden than ever before, in the ruins of their beautiful city where law and order have ceased to exist. And what is the prize that is to be eventually won? The rebirth of democracy. The glorious prospect of being able one day to choose their rulers from a list of powerful men, most of whose corruptions are generally known and accepted with weary resignation. The days of Benito Mussolini must seem like a lost paradise compared with this.

September 25

Neil Armstrong, on his way back to Bari, brought messages from HQ. It is eighteen months since we parted company in Tunisia, since which he has been through the whole of the Italian campaign, beginning with Sicily. Seeing him again, I realize how totally he has changed, and how completely Southern Italy has taken over and transformed this Englishman. Nowadays I would take him for an Italian disguised in a British uniform; one of the lean and silent kind who speak in meaningful grunts, and a play of hands with which they build up their thoughts, like a potter at his wheel. We carried our wicker chairs to the doorway of the hotel and surveyed the Benevento scene, sipping an apéritif of marsala while a black-market meal was being put together. Sun crackled on the walls. A man who, incredibly in this environment of searing drought, repaired umbrellas for a living, emitted in passing us the despairing howl which is the call of his trade. The finest hearse in all the province – carved all over with angels and cupids of silver and gold – rumbled past drawn by eight black horses to pick up some victim of the pest. Two *scugnizzi* came into sight in pursuit of a crippled cat, whose death would furnish their meagre lives with a moment of pleasure.

We swapped stories and boasted about the burdens we were carrying in our respective places of exile. I mentioned the case of the vanishing corpse outside the Café Roma. '*Eh già*,' Armstrong said. It was one of those meaningless Italian expressions that served for comments of all kinds, but was a vehicle for resignation. I watched the once straightforward English face which a year of solitary confinement in the heel of Italy had turned into such a marvellous barometer of wariness and scepticism. When one of the regulars came through the door and passed us muttering a polite *ossequi*, Armstrong's eyes swivelled cautiously, and although his hand did not move, I almost expected him to grope for his testicles.

Benevento, he had come to the conclusion, was a poor sort of place compared to Bari, and he was sorry to see me marooned here. The towns of the far South had been less smashed up in the war, and as the drains went on working there were few cases of the typhoid and smallpox that scourged the Naples area. People killed each other down there for reasons of their own as they did here, but Armstrong had learned to keep out of involvements of this kind. He had also learned to cope with the local Carabinieri marshals, though he agreed that few of them demonstrated the kind of sinister power possessed by Altamura.

There were two messages for me; one requesting information on the activities of Maresciallo Altamura for transmission to Major Pecorella in Naples, the second calling for investigation of an alleged rape.

The rape had been committed by an unidentified member of the Allied forces, and on reading this my heart sank. If any soldier had raped a woman in Benevento, the chances that this would have been one of the Canadians were strong. The lady, one Irene Imbrosi, occupied a flat in the Corso Umberto in a block where men of substance housed their lady-loves. Irene received me in a well-furnished room with a religious atmosphere provided by several plaster saints and an ugly model in silver of the Cathedral of Milan. She was majestic in true Southern style, with a cataract of black hair, the eyes of a tragedienne and the innocence of expression that completes the armament of any outstanding harlot.

There was something mysterious about this complaint, seeming to fly in the face of local prejudice. Rape is a fairly everyday event in this part of the world, and is not necessarily a serious business for the victim. Peasant girls in some of the big estates are raped by their overseers as a matter of course every day of the week. It is said that a local count provides members of his work force to any male guest who visits the *latifundia* for a riding or shooting holiday, his sole stipulation being not to spoil them with gifts of money. Concealment of what has happened is what matters, to avoid a personal slump in value in the sexual market. Why had Irene reported her experience to her lover, a *barone* who owned half a million olive trees, who, by-passing the local authorities, had gone straight to AMG in Naples with his complaint?

Irene's story of her attack was that an unknown soldier had seen her in the street, followed her home, forced his way into the flat which he said he had authority to search, found a cache of army blankets, and then perpetrated the rape. 'Everybody has army blankets,' she said. 'You couldn't go through a single flat in the building without finding some.' And this was true.

I asked if she had any marks on her body to show a doctor, if necessary, as evidence that violence was used, and she didn't think so.

There seemed to be no real anger in her at the memory of the outrage she had suffered, and her indignation lacked conviction. She could give no description of her assailant that might have led to the identification of any man of flesh and blood. The description of the man who had pounced on Irene, carried her through into the bedroom, and flung her on to the bed sounded like that of any of the anonymous, faceless suspects sent to us by No. 3 District for inclusion in the Black Book: average height, age, size and colour – she couldn't even be quite sure whether or not he had a moustache. Twice she said, 'I don't want to cause any trouble for anyone,' and had to be reminded of the seriousness of the charge.

Finally I decided to ask her what had made her tell the Baron about the attack, and after some embarrassment, side-stepping and self-contradiction, the truth began to filter through. The rape turned out to have been prolonged, almost a leisurely affair, occupying some hours, and the Baron, happening to have decided to visit his mistress on that afternoon, had arrived on the scene only minutes after the soldier had hitched up his trousers and gone his way. He had taken note of the condition of the bedroom, and then the bed, and been compelled to draw conclusions. A good and religious man – a leader of the nascent Christian Democratic Party – he had accepted Irene's account of her misadventure without question and had no blame for her, but had felt himself unable to continue their affair. Out of the generosity of his heart, she said, he had then produced a suggestion: namely, that should it be possible to track down the soldier involved and persuade him to take Irene in marriage, he would make a handsome settlement in their favour.

This, then, was the situation in a nutshell. If any presentable Allied soldier could be tempted to come forward, admit to the rape of Irene, and agree to marry her, he could expect a wedding-present of a quarter of a million lire along with his beautiful wife. Hence Irene's determination not to provide a description which might fail to tally with that of an acceptable candidate.

This appeared to me quite likely to have been a plot staged

by the Baron to disengage himself from the liaison in a graceful fashion, and with good conscience. Anything could happen in Benevento.

October 6

After duty visits to Ischia and Rome I returned to Naples today, and am back in the Riviere di Chiaia until further notice. Here I found a great accumulation of work. The fact is that we are far too thin on the ground to be dispersed outside the city in the way we have been. In addition, the Section has been weakened by sickness, Moore with hepatitis and Parkinson with a mysterious and chronic infection of the liver. However, both work on with unabated vigour. Two other members suffer from intense depression, and I have had malaria for the third time.

Overwork has certainly contributed to this general decline in health. One is tempted by the strangeness and excitement of the life, by the fascination of this legalized eavesdropping on humanity in which we are continually involved, to work on regardless of the clock. I have frequently found myself occupied in Section activities for up to 15 hours a day, and on three occasions lately have fallen asleep at the wheel of a car — once while driving the Canadians' Dodge, in which — at two in the morning — I mounted a traffic island in Naples and snapped off a lamp standard.

The news from Benevento is that Marshal Altamura has been charged by the order of Major Pecorella with irregularities and withdrawn from service there, doubtless to the relief of that long-suffering town.

October 8

A most embarrassing episode happened today. Mobs of youths gathered in the gardens of the Villa Nazionale, overlooked by the front windows of our palazzo, and began to assault girls found in the company of Allied soldiers. The girls were chased up and down the gardens, and when caught their knickers were torn off. Soldiers who intervened to defend their girls were promptly beaten up. We heard a few distant yells, saw running figures, but no more. A few minutes later No. 3 District was on the phone to the FSO ordering us out into the streets to keep order. Once again it's evident that nobody knows what we're really supposed to be doing here. This time we seem to be seen as a sort of watered-down version of the SS. Yet over and over again we've been told it is not our job to take over the duties of the Italian police.

When this order came through there happened to be four of us at HQ, and the order was to arm ourselves with Thompson sub-machine-guns and go out and do whatever was necessary. The sub-machine-guns turned up a few weeks back, after we'd gone through the active part of the campaign with our pistols and our original five rounds of ammunition apiece. No one has fired a single shot, either with the pistols or the sub-machine-guns, which were examined with a certain amount of respect when delivered, and then put away and forgotten about. Now the four of us who happened to be caught in this predicament were actually obliged to grab one of these imposing weapons apiece, see to it that it was properly loaded, try to remember how it worked, and then sally forth into the Riviera di Chiaia, trying to look like British Army versions of Al Capone, but ready to duck down the nearest side street and disappear from the scene at the first sign of trouble.

Fortunately for us there was no trouble. Approaching the danger spot with extreme caution and taking full advantage of the cover offered by tree-trunks, bushes and the occasional statue, all we found was as calm and pacific a scene as one could hope to find in any municipal gardens on a sunny afternoon. The storm had come and passed. The sellers of sweets and nuts had settled peacefully at their stalls. All the local black-market activities, involving the sale of American cigarettes, articles of military clothing and food, were being carried on with absolute normality. A nursemaid dressed in an amazing Victorian uniform with a lace cap and white gloves was playing ball with a little girl in ribbons and bows who looked like a kewpie doll, and a drunken American Negro slept in a flower-bed. We could go home.

The incident highlighted an unhappy and deteriorating situation produced by the encroachment of the Allied presence on the emotional and romantic life of the city. Naples, the world's largest village, is divided into many smaller villages, the *rioni*, each one of which is in effect an enormous family. In each of these quite literally every member is known to every other member, and the circumstances and history of every family are a matter of public knowledge. Marriages, on the whole, tend to take place within the *rione*, and in the case of some – for example the fishermen's quarter, the Pallonetta di Santa Lucia – the young person of either sex hardly ever marries an outsider. Each *rione* has its web of relationships, its traditions, its social structure, and betrothal and marriage are the concern of all.

Then the foreign soldiers came on the scene and were in immediate collision with the local boys, who had no work, no prestige, no money, absolutely nothing to offer the girls. A British private, wretchedly paid as he is, earns more than a foreman at the Navale Meccanica, while an American private – who can shower cigarettes, sweets, and even silk stockings in all directions – has a higher income than any Italian employee in Naples. The temptation is very great, and few seem able to resist. Thus the long, delicate, intricate business of the old Neapolitan courtship – as complex as the mating ritual of exotic birds – is replaced by a brutal, wordless approach, and a crude act of purchase. One wonders how long it will take the young of Naples, after we have gone, to recover from the bitterness of this experience.

Last week a young American soldier of Polish parentage called

at our HQ to say that he had just been to a party in Mari-
chiaro where he believed a man purporting to be a Polish
officer was a spy, as he clearly had little knowledge of the part
of Poland he claimed to come from. I drove him back to the
party in the FSO's car, and we went in and talked to the man.
My conclusion was that he probably was a spy, but it was
better to do nothing about it, because had I arrested him and
it turned out that a mistake had been made, all the wrath of
the Polish army would have been called down on my head,
and my head alone.

We therefore set out on our way back. After we had driven
a few yards the American said, 'I feel like a woman. How
about trying that house over there?' He showed me his haver-
sack containing several cans of meat, and asked to be put
down outside an apartment building – one of a dozen in sight.
I waited while he rang the bell, and put his proposition to
whoever it was came to the door. Then he waved back to
me to carry on, and went in.

October 10

In September in Naples it usually rains torrentially for a few
days, after which benefit of water the fields in October put on
strong new greens in replacement of the brown desolation of
summer. The sunshine of this month charges the landscape
with deep, solid colour, but the heat is gone. It is the habit
of Neapolitans to go on family outings whenever they can
at this time of the year. These excursions in the fine, fresh,
lively days of autumn are called *ottobrate*. The woods are full
of chestnuts, fungi spring up out of the damp earth, and edible
plants of the order of dandelions and plantains, for use in
salads, sprout among the new grass. People go out in their
thousands – mainly at the weekends – in search of these wild
delicacies. This is also the time when flocks of small migrant
birds pass through, going southwards on their way to winter
in Africa, and there is no bird insignificant enough to escape

the interest of the sportsmen that lie in wait for them with guns and nets in the fields and the orchards all round the city.

By invitation of Ingeniere Crespi, with whom I have been on good terms since the episode of the leakage of information over Anzio, I took part yesterday, Sunday, in a family expedition to collect *funghi* and salad plants, and to try our luck with the migrant birds at the Lago di Patria, some ten miles along the coast to the west of Naples. We went in two cars, the Ingeniere, his eighteen-year-old son, Andrea, and myself in one, and Signora Crespi, a nephew and his wife in the second. As Crespi and his son proposed to shoot duck – or failing that, anything that flew – they were fantastically dressed in green knickerbockers and Alpine hats. Signora Crespi wore a costume in Scotch tartan of a fierce design from Milan. She and her party were after mushrooms and greenstuff, and to avoid confusion between edible fungi and others of extreme similarity of appearance which are deadly, they had brought with them an enormous rolled-up coloured poster to be used in carrying on comparisons in the field.

We arrived at the lake in less than an hour, having passed other families already busy in the fields, cutting dandelions and stuffing them in paper bags. The report was that as there had been no duck-shooting last autumn in this area – which had been fought over as the Germans withdrew to the line of the Volturno – the sporting expectations were bright. Signora Crespi and party were left at the edge of a small pine-wood where the nephew had already spotted glistening yellow toadstools, towards which they ran carrying their poster, and uttering cries of delight. The rest of us carried on a mile or so to the shores of the lake.

Here the prospects seemed dismal. We stood, the Crespis holding their splendid guns, looking out over a surface of water that was as clean as a newly polished mirror. Another party of sportsmen mooched into sight on the far side of the lake, then disappeared again. A peasant came up and offered to show Crespi where edible frogs could be taken, but his offer was declined. The lake was bordered by sedge which Andrea was determined to investigate. He went off, returning in about an hour slimed to the knees in mud, and carrying a handful of feathers trailing green legs, which had once been a moorhen. This was success. Father and son hugged each other with delight. A moorhen wasn't a duck, but it was the next best thing.

Andrea cleaned up as best he could and we drove back to where we'd left the rest of the family, who'd done reasonably well with the fungi, with a fair collection scraped from tree-trunks or discovered – revealed by their startling colours – among the black rotting pine needles. There was a joyful out-cry at the sight of the moorhen, and kisses and more hugs for Andrea from the womenfolk. After that the fungus-gatherers were deserted once again and we drove off over a sunken road to a particularly good position Crespi knew of. There were areas, he said – and this was one of them – where migrant birds seemed inclined to pause and to hover, as if to get their bearings. He spoke of people who sometimes brought small trees with them, covered them with bird-lime, and stuck them into the ground here – sure of a good catch, although he personally saw not much fun or skill in the practice. His own favoured device was a piece of Heath-Robinson equipment carried in sections in the boot of the car. This, when assembled, looked like a model oil-derrick, with a rotating top encrusted with pieces of mirror set at different angles, which, when in motion flashed into the sky, attracted the curiosity of passing birds, and brought them within range.

This contraption was set up near an isolated bush, where it would be convenient for tired and inquisitive birds to alight. Strings attached to the rotating head were stretched back to where we crouched in the deep road in hiding behind the car, and were wound by Andrea over a bobbin to set the thing in motion. We were in the middle of a vast field with flowering spikes of asphodel thrusting up from the grass all round, and in the middle distance the blackened debris of a German half-track. Our first success was with a lark, drawn out of the sky as if by a magnet, and destroyed by Crespi's impeccable shot. There followed buntings, more larks, wheatears, chats, black-caps and five or six neat grey-green half-ounces of warbler, hardly any of them spoiled to the eye by the tiny, specially prepared shot with which Crespi had filled his cartridges in preparation for this delicate slaughter. Although these birds must have hailed from the north, they all appeared slightly different from our English version of similar species. Only a local goldfinch, alighting on the bush with a burst of brief twittering song before extermination, was totally familiar.

The final bag was eighteen small corpses having a total weight perhaps of a pound. Crespi regarded this as a success, and an excellent return for the expenditure in ammunition and effort. The passion for hunting, he said, could come even before the pursuit of love, and be equally remote from the balance sheets of gain or loss. Ferdinand of Naples had spent the equivalent of several million pounds on building his palace at Capodimonte just because this hill was on the route of migrating *beccafiche* – warblers of all kinds – and having finished the palace, a road to Naples had to be built at the cost of another million or two. It was estimated, said Crespi, that every warbler eaten by the royal sportsmen cost the nation a thousand ducats.

We joined up with the rest of the family by the edge of the wood, picnicked off salami, mortadella and mozzarella cheese, the latter warranted to have been produced from the authentic milk of the buffaloes raised in the swamps of the Volturno, and which in appearance and vascular rubbery texture attempts to imitate the testicles of these beasts. After that, it was back to Naples, dizzy with success. It had been, as all agreed, an excellent day's sport. I delicately extricated myself from the invitation to dinner that evening.

October 16

A number of weeks of hard work on the part of Robert Parkinson culminated today in an operation mounted at the Pace Hospital for women.

Parkinson's most valuable contact in Naples has been Professore Placella, the gynæcologist specializing in the restoration of lost virginity for all who can afford it, who is also a consultant at the hospital. Goodness knows what Parkinson has been able to do for Placella, who is as subject to the laws of Omertà as is any other Neapolitan in a case affecting his own colleagues. Whatever it is, it has induced the Professore to supply the hint or the clue to the reason for our failure to cope with the epidemic of VD.

This afternoon British and American MPs descended on a dozen clubs, dance-halls and bars – even on the cafés in the Galleria – arrested every woman in sight, and carried them off to the Pace for examination. This has happened before on a smaller and less vigorous scale. The procedure is that vaginal smears are taken in each case, and those found to be clear of infection are released forthwith, while VD sufferers are forcibly detained for hospital treatment, as long as may be necessary.

With Placella's help a trap had been set, but owing to the importance of the case Parkinson felt that this was an occasion when it might be useful to have a witness present, and I was invited to go along. We went to the hospital, were quietly admitted by a back entrance, put on surgeons' coats over our uniforms, and were then introduced to the smiling and bowing Assistant Director of the hospital as British Army Medical staff who were paying a routine visit to observe the method employed in carrying out examinations of cases of suspected venereal disease.

The inspections were to take place in an enormous room furnished with a row of gynæcological chairs. As soon as we arrived and joined the group of Italian doctors there, the detained women began to stream in like sheep about to be hustled through a dip. In most cases they were dressed with a respectable formality that seemed to intensify the indignity to which they were to be subjected. The operation moved at the pace of a bull-fight. The first six women, some of them sobbing and protesting, were led forward, ordered to remove their knickers, pull up their skirts, and settle themselves in the chairs in which their legs, held in stirrups, were grotesquely raised and separated. At the door a constantly increasing group kept up a frantic argument. Among them were a few bejewelled courtesans and some obvious bar-girls, but the majority looked like young housewives, some with their shopping-bags on their arms, and there were some very young girls who were certain to be virgins. A suspicion grew that over-enthusiastic MPs had not been above snatching girls at random off the street.

The doctors went to work with their speculums and swabs while the great, bare, grimy *sala* resounded with the noise of weeping. Parkinson, Placella and I walked dutifully past the exposed pudenda, nodding our satisfaction at the work, waited while another row of victims, knickers in hand, faces streaming with tears, took their places, then returned. Occasionally Placella would stop with a cry of pretended astonishment to point out to us some collector's item of a chancre. An ugly and most depressing experience.

Success of the scheme depended on the vindication of Parkinson's theory that two prostitutes known to be infected with syphilis, who had been carefully included in this round-up, would be able to bribe their way out, and this they did. They were immediately arrested and freely admitted that they, as well as other infected women, had been approached by a hospital underling known in the half-world of Naples as *sciacquapalle* (balls-rinser). This man arranged for the supply of a certificate of good health on the payment, through him, of 10,000 lire to the hospital's Assistant Director.

Professore Placella estimated that in this way about three infected prostitutes a day had been released from the Pace, and that each one could be responsible for as many as 5000 new cases of VD annually. Thanks to Parkinson's efforts, this particular hole in the dyke will be stopped. The forms are being typed out for the Assistant Director's arrest tomorrow. The Germans would shoot him, and they would be right to do so. As it is, he has been able to buy friendship and support in AMG – now almost totally corrupt – so in due course he will come to trial and almost certainly get off.

October 20

I am concerned at the increasing number of applications by officers or other ranks to marry Italian civilians. COs must realize that everything possible will be done to discourage such marriages, few of which turn out happily or even survive more than a short period. Statistics of last war marriages with foreigners prove that only 5% turned out successful. There is no reason to hope that present war international marriages will prove any more satisfactory. The reverse is more likely, owing to the even more bitter feeling to which it has given rise. After the last war there were many cases of men who could not stand the unhappiness of their wives and children any longer, and went to live in the wife's country, usually to their unending regret. In all cases the wife forced them to do so. It is the duty of all officers to protect our troops from matrimonial shipwreck. It should be pointed out that the soldier has no future security to offer his wife. He is at present a temporary government employee, and the future is dependent upon obtaining a suitable permanent job in civilian life. No one can marry with impunity upon such a basis. There are many other differences which, although small in themselves, such as different tastes as regards cooking, do militate strongly against happiness.

This circular issued by the GOC, No. 3 District, dated 5 September 1944, is probably the real reason behind the sudden coming to an end of my investigation into the suitability of marriages proposed between the British soldiery and Italian girls in the Naples area. In the first three months 43 such vettings have been carried out, and in 12 cases the report has been favourable. Recently, however much the General may complain of the increased rate of application, few have come my way. I suspect that pressure has been put upon soldiers to change their minds, and that in some cases the men have been quietly posted out of the area. However this may be, I am out of it for good, having been relieved by the FSO of this particular duty in so subtle a fashion that I'm bound to suspect that after a year of close contact with the seamy side of life in Naples he's been unable to avoid infection by the deviousness of the environment.

Three days ago I was sent to vet Liana Pagano, living at Via Aniello Falcone 32; a widow, aged 22, mother dead, father mechanic working at Navale Meccanico (never inscribed in Fascist Party), one sister married into the family of a priest, one still at school, was born and has always lived in Naples, has one child, speaks English slightly, is not pregnant. In other words an apparently respectable girl, from a respectable lower-class background – the fact that a sister is married into a priest's family being an important factor in the family's standing and its morale.

Liana was cheerful, fresh-faced (no make-up), and full of bustling, darting movement. She lived in two bare, scoured and whitewashed rooms over *bassi* occupied by families one rung lower down in the social scale, and had with her a sparkling black-eyed boy of four, almost as big as herself. The Commisario at the local *stazione*, visited in advance, confirmed that there was no record, and speaking of her the scheming, predatory features seemed to soften a little. She was 'as good as bread', he said, and suddenly I noticed for the first time that the Neapolitans show a reverence for bread greater even than for gold.

Her husband, Liana told me, had been killed in the war. She showed me a jaunty card sent from Cyrenaica the day before he had gone into a desert battle, to be seen no more. Africa, as she put it, had eaten him up. A photograph, the cell-like room's only decoration, showed him buttoned into his tight uniform with his fine, young, up-swept moustache, and his feathered hat. He had been in the Wolves of Tuscany — once a crack unit before the hurricane of war had swept it away. Now she was in love with a REME sergeant, who sounded a sedate fellow and was virtually certain to survive. She needed a father for her boy, she said.

I asked her the key question — on what did she live? She showed me the doeskin gloves she made for sale in the shops in the Via Roma. Her income from this was the equivalent of about one pound a week. In the spring and the autumn, she said, she helped out on a cousin's farm at Casoria, hoeing in spring and helping with the apple harvest in autumn. For this she received a little more — the equivalent of 25s. a week — but the work was hard, fourteen hours a day. October is the best of the year in Southern Italy. We went out on to the balcony into the mild sunshine. All round us were white walls, gloriously sculpted and dimpled by light. Women were hanging out washing above and below, and snatches came from them of the sweet songs composed in the slum of Santa Lucia all round us. It was a moment of poetry. 'Do what you can for me,' she said, and I promised I would and went away to compose the kind of subdued and matter-of-fact report that was best calculated to further Liana's cause.

Having read this, the FSO proceeded to put his plan into action by sending for my friend, that investigatory tiger, Robert Parkinson, and telling him to vet the girl. Parkinson was taken by surprise, knowing that I normally dealt with all marriage vettings, but was unable to confer with me, because I'd been found a job taking me out into the country, the idea possibly being to keep me out of the way.

The choice of Parkinson was probably deliberate, and reflected the fact that the FSO was in no doubt now as to the divergence in our attitudes towards Italy and Italians. A year among the Italians had converted me to such an admiration for their humanity and culture that I realize that were I given the chance to be born again and to choose the place of my birth, Italy would be the country of my choice.

Not so Parkinson. It was a curious fact that of all of us Robert might have achieved the deepest penetration of Italian life, and yet in his way remained aloof from it. All his free time was spent with his Italian friends. He spoke the language with a kind of grave rectitude, quoted Leopardi, sent cards and flowers on people's saint's day, and presents for their children on the Feast of Epiphany. Like Eric Williams, he could stand at a window in our first-floor headquarters and conduct a basic conversation with someone in the Via Calabritto below purely by movements of the head and hands. In other words, almost an Italian. Italy and Italians fascinated him. He enjoyed, as we all did, the intrigue – games we all played together. He was enchanted by the genial trickeries of our environment. His curiosity was endlessly stimulated, but I felt his love was never awakened. He would find it harder than I do to give an Italian the benefit of the doubt.

Robert, as instructed, went off to see Liana, who must have been surprised to receive two military visitors in one day. He would have sat on the same low hard chair on which I had sat, bleakly enduring the asceticism of his surroundings, immune to Liana's gamine charm, noting that the whole equipment of living in the apartment, apart from a table, two chairs and a bed, was kept in a single battered tin trunk. This penury he would compare in his mind's eye with the REME sergeant's probable background of dinner services and matching suites. He might have glanced at the photo of the Wolf of Tuscany whose vanished arrogance would have seemed to him contemptible rather than pathetic. He would undoubtedly have registered the siting of the lavatory, as so often is the case, behind a sort of stable door in the tiny area of the living-room serving as a kitchen.

There is an inherent Mediterranean austerity much in evidence in the Naples area, in Sorrento and Capri, which seems to come from the sea, since it is hardly to be found inland. This expresses itself in a taste for unadorned spaces, and is the visual equivalent of intervals of silence. I suspected that Parkinson found this emptiness of design alien and repellent, and that there would have been no appeal in Liana's spotless linen hanging on the balcony, her whitewashed walls and the scrubbed floor tiles where linoleum should have been. He would have questioned her in his slow, deliberate way, like a counsel for the prosecution, snapped his notebook with awful finality, bowed and gone away. When the FSO called me in and read out the two reports no one would have believed that they could have had to do with the same girl. So Liana will not get her British husband, and I will be doing no more marriage vettings. With the combined efforts of the GOC and Sergeant Parkinson, there will be few international marriages from now on in this area.

October 24

The thunderbolt has fallen. Today I was ordered to prepare to leave immediately for Taranto, to embark on the *Reina del Pacifico* for Port Said, where I am to pick up 3000 Russian soldiers who had been fighting with the Germans and gone over to the Partisans. These are to be repatriated, evidently with discretion, to the Soviet Union, via the Red Sea, the Persian Gulf and Khorramshahr in Iran. Instructions are, as usual, vague to the point of cryptic. The AFHQ order reads, 'You will be away as long as necessary,' but does not define the duties to be performed.

My intuition warns me that my stay in Naples has come to an end, a surmise reinforced by the FSO's mention of the near-certainty that as soon as this mission is completed I shall be posted for liaison duties with the Russians on the Eastern Front.

So I am left with only hours to spare and no time to say goodbye to any of the friends scattered through so many towns. There will be no time for a last glass of marsala with any of the scheming sindacos or the Machiavellian chiefs of police, who have always, for all their innumerable short-comings, shown hospitality to me as a stranger. There will be no time for a last coffee substitute in the Gran Caffè in the Galleria to say goodbye and good luck to several girls who are virtually fixtures of the place, and bear me no ill-will because I was unable to help them to marry Allied personnel. I realize that I have had my last meal at 'Zi' Teresa's and will never again shake the gnarled paw of the old aunt herself, as she sits behind the showcase full of octopus and crabs, trying to pick out the sound of her cash-register bell from the music of the house troubadors. There won't be even a half-hour to spare for a dash up to the Vomero for a last panoramic view across the gardens of the Villa Floridiana of the great grey and red city spread below, presenting at this distance a totally fallacious aspect of dignified calm; or for a final contemplation of the somnolent Vesuvius, so changed in outline since its reshaping by the eruption.

Instead, with a foretaste of the nostalgia to come, I have to make do with what is on the spot. I do my packing in the bedroom, trying as I do so to imprint on my memory all the details of the piazza, admiring for the last time the statuary: Proserpine – her bottom pocked by some tommy-gunner's high-spirited fire – being carried off by Pluto; Hercules at grips with the Hydra. In the background I watch the sea charging up the anthracite beach.

Into the office to gather my papers together and write the day's report, realizing with sorrow how many projects have been started but will now never be completed. A movement at a window across the road distracts me and I look up to see a woman called Giulietta appear momentarily between the shutters naked from the waist up on the pretence of washing herself – a familiar sight which we have come to accept as no more than a tiny offering to the god of fertility. A seller of brooms passes below in the street with a cry like a muezzin calling the faithful to prayer. Evening meals are already being prepared, and the smell of the miracle of good cooking thrusts back for a moment that of drains. For the last time I look into the eyes of the enormous and enigmatic female statues flanking the entrance to the Calabritto Palace, and then into the court-yard itself, where a small child is pissing into the mouth of a stone lion.

Perhaps when everything is ready for the move off – at 6.30 a.m. tomorrow from the Stazione Centrale – there will at least be a moment left to call on Lattarullo, most faithful of my Neapolitan allies. I know in advance that, having staggered under the impact of the news and then recovered with proper fortitude, he will whisper, 'I've got a treat for you.' This he will describe as *caccia* – game – but it will be a muscled city pigeon netted on someone's roof. He will dash out to find the neighbourhood girl, who will stew it in garlic and herbs and serve it up on the great ancestral salver. When it is time to go he will take my hand and say, 'I'll be at the station tomorrow, to see you off,' and I know he will be there as promised, dressed in all the dignity of his 'Zio di Roma' suit for such an occasion.